Enjoy your time coloring..
Let go from the world..
Take your time..
Relax your mind..

———————

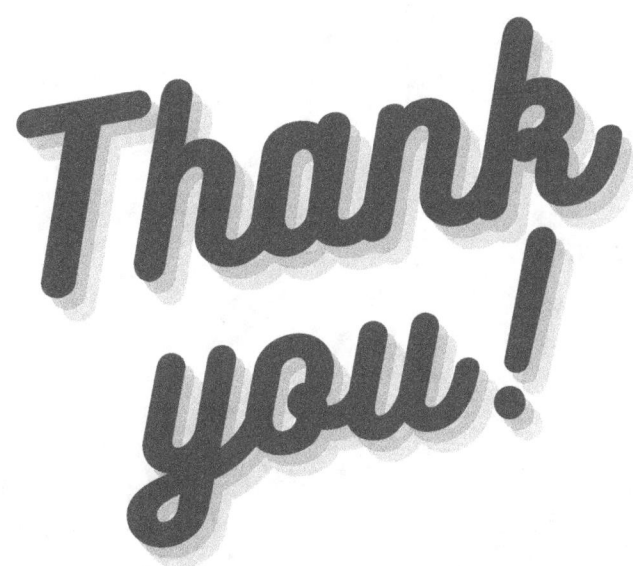

This Book Belongs to:

_____

aka: the best person ever

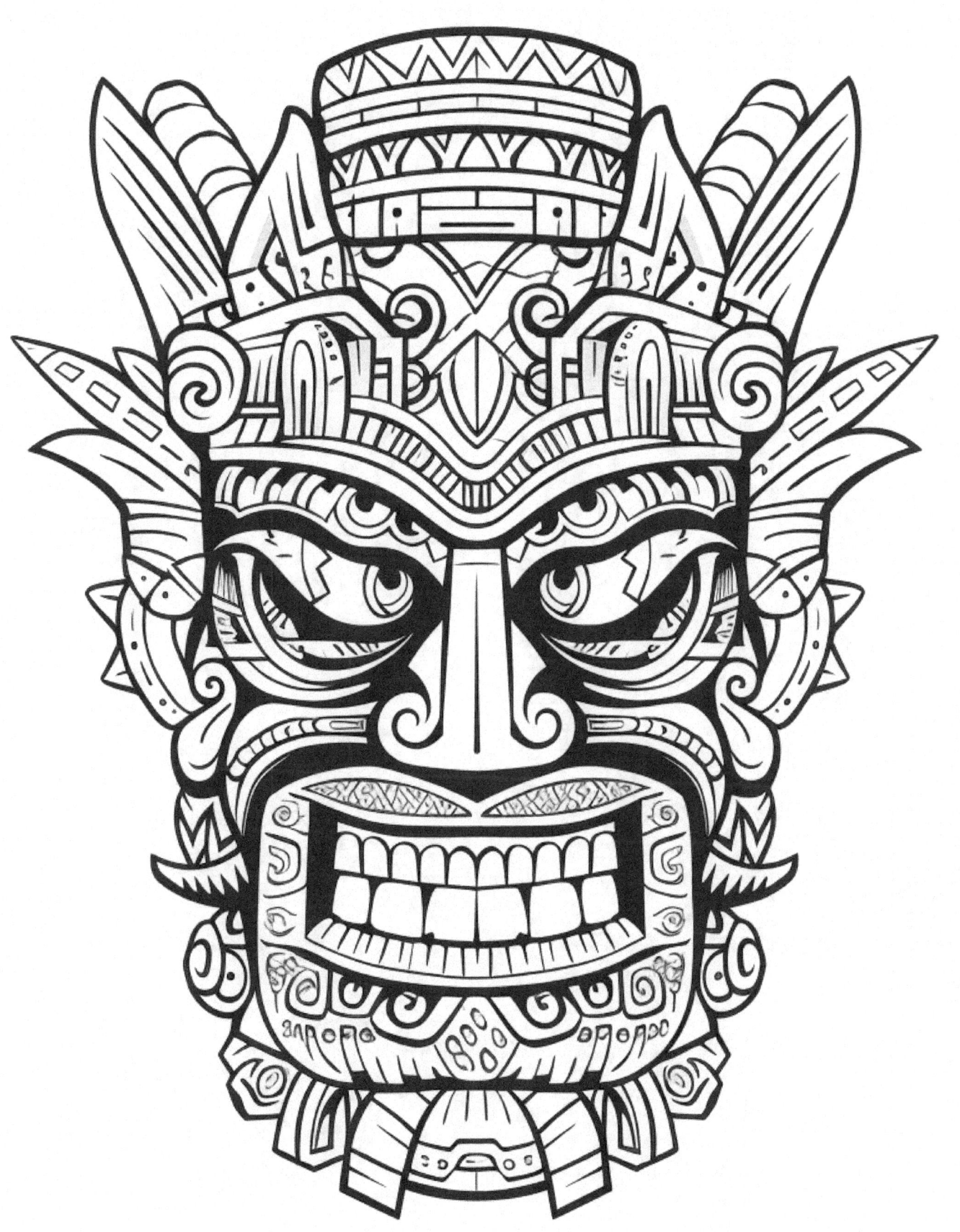

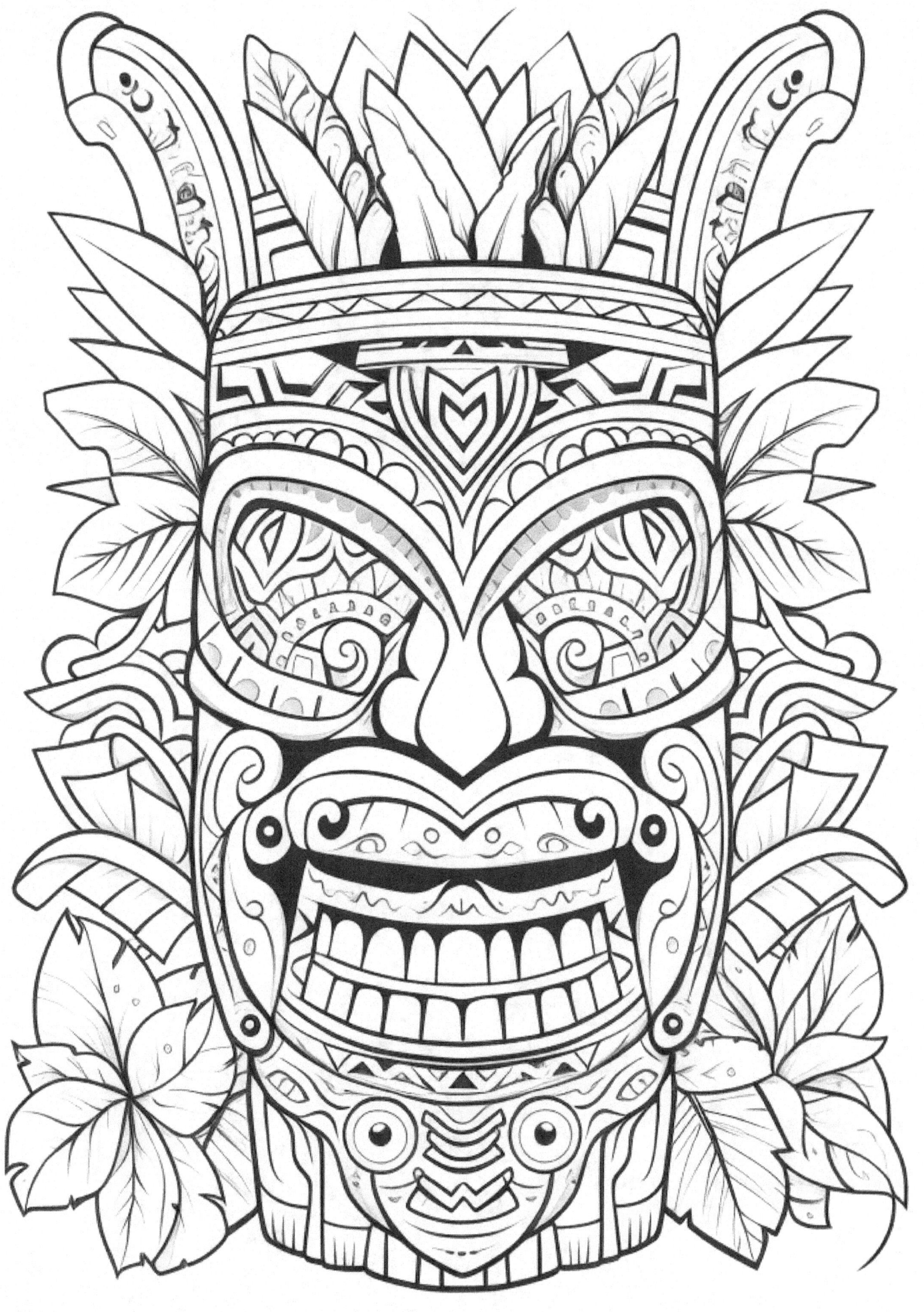

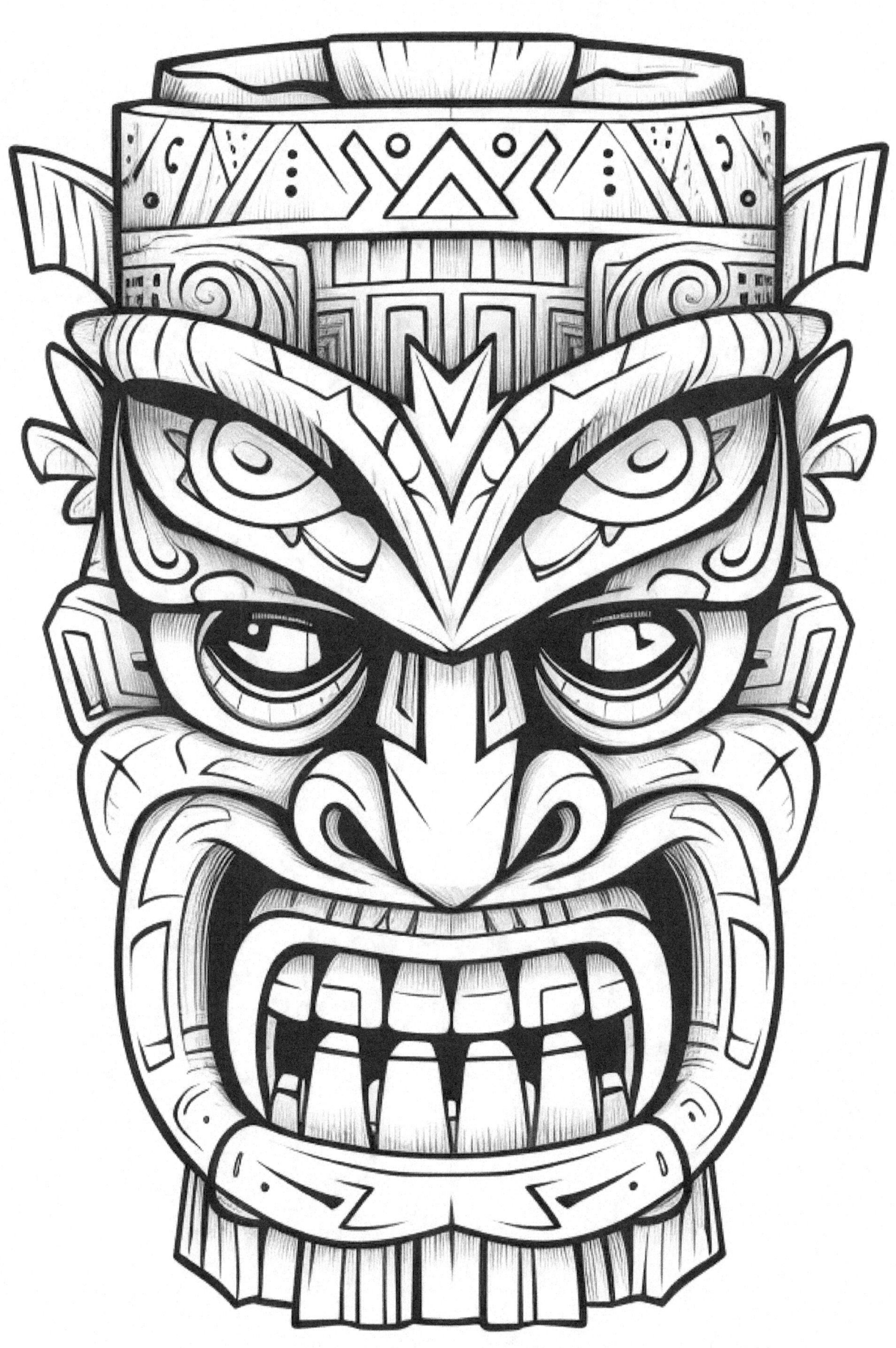

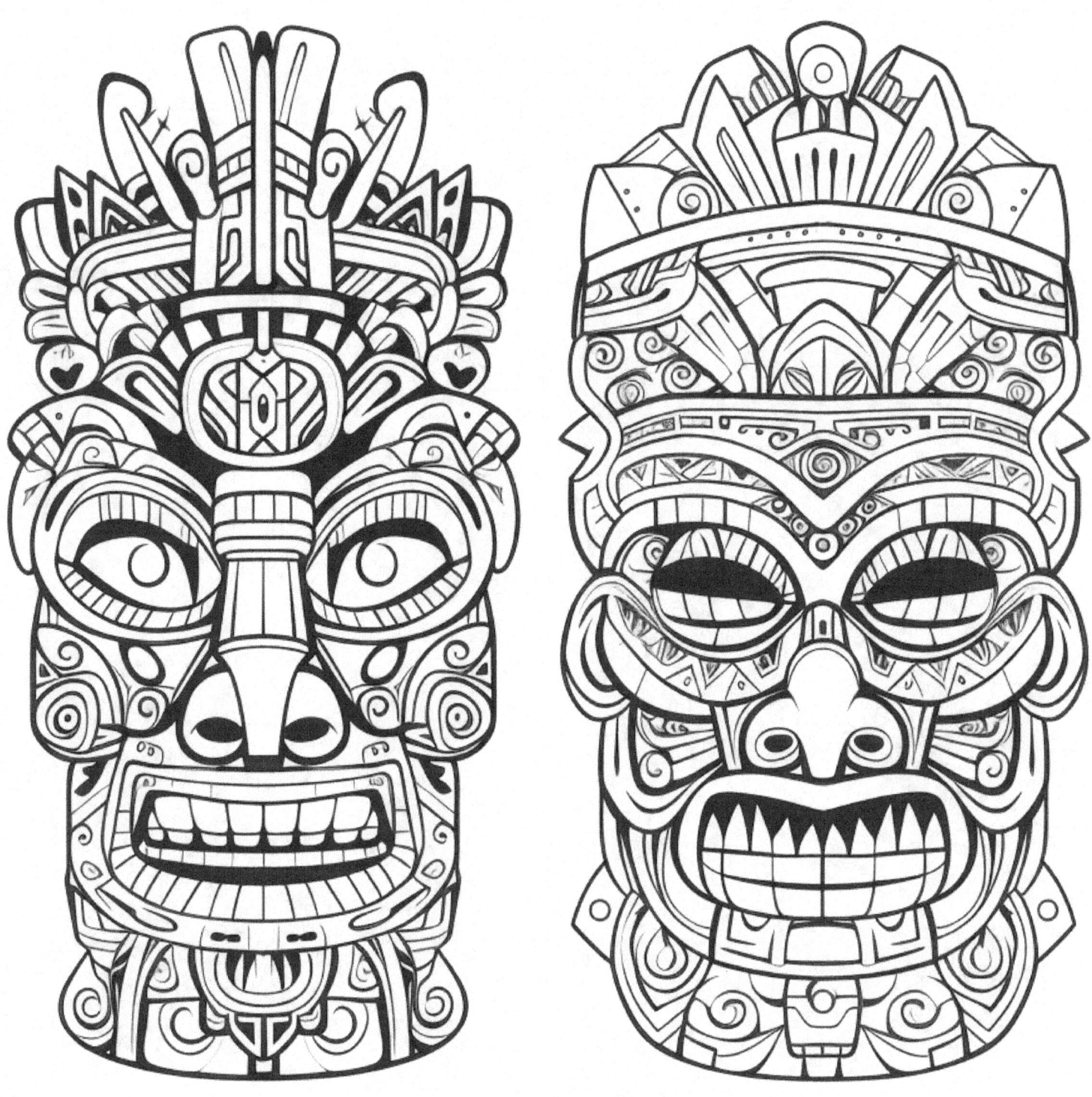

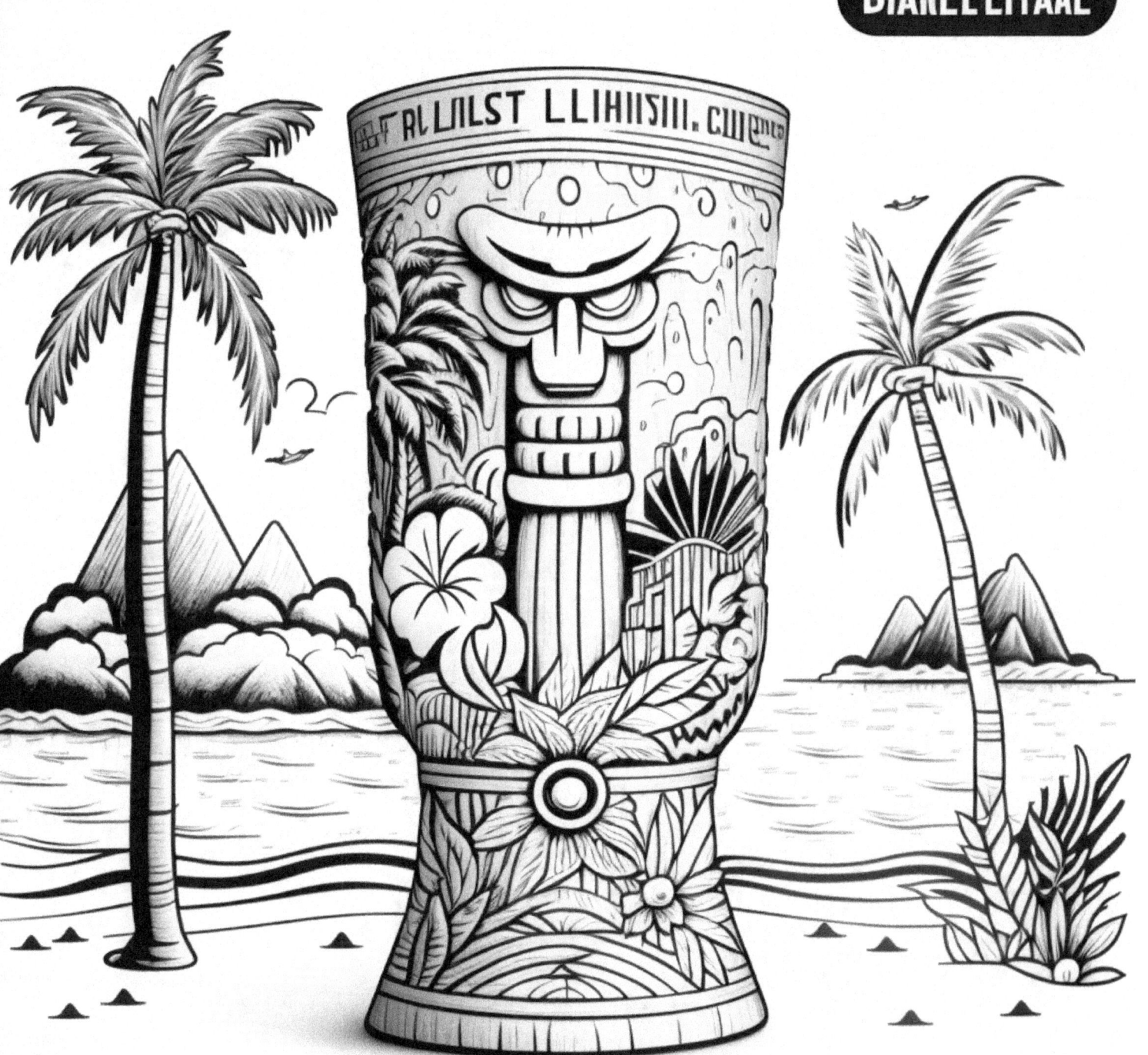

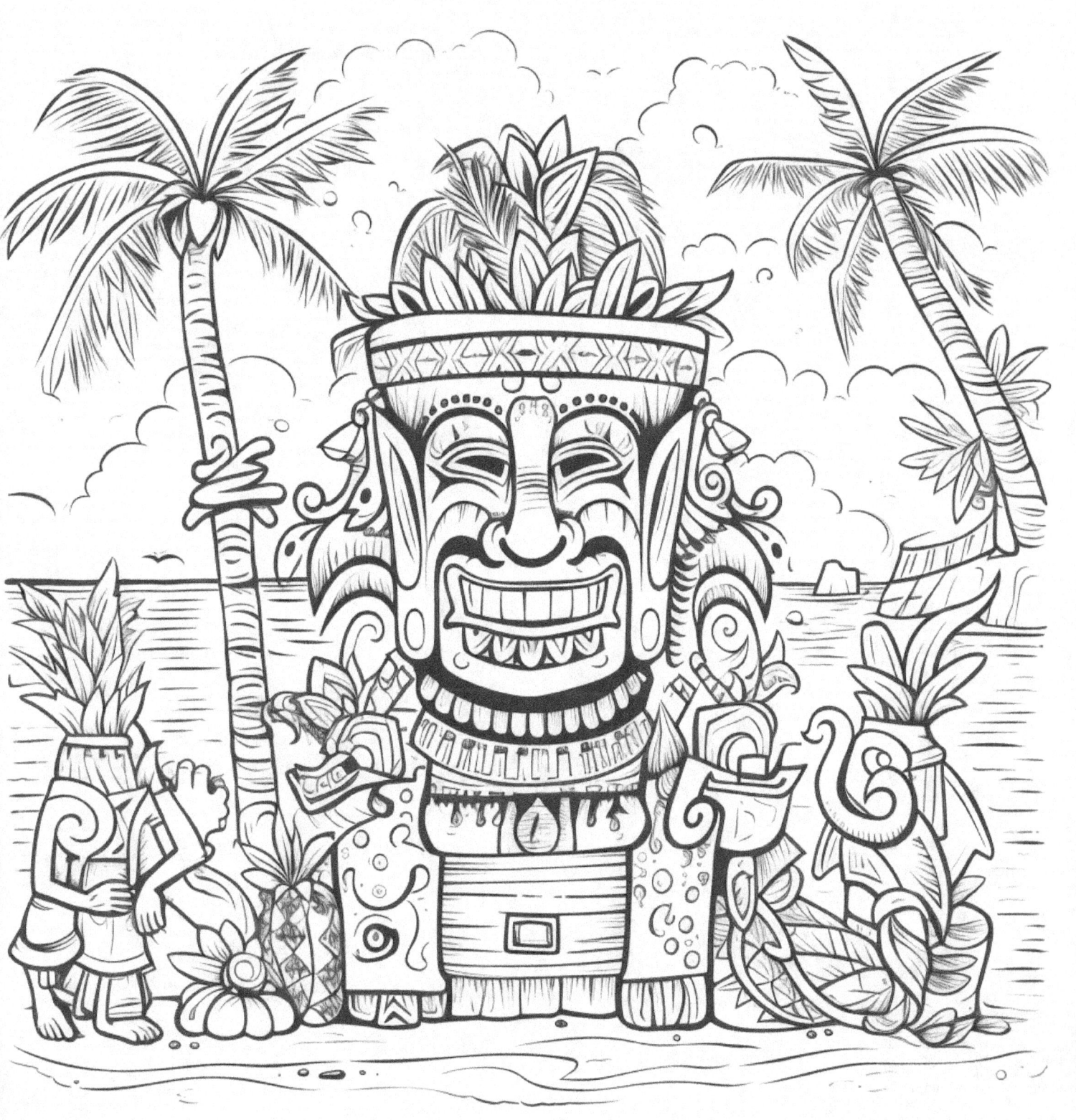

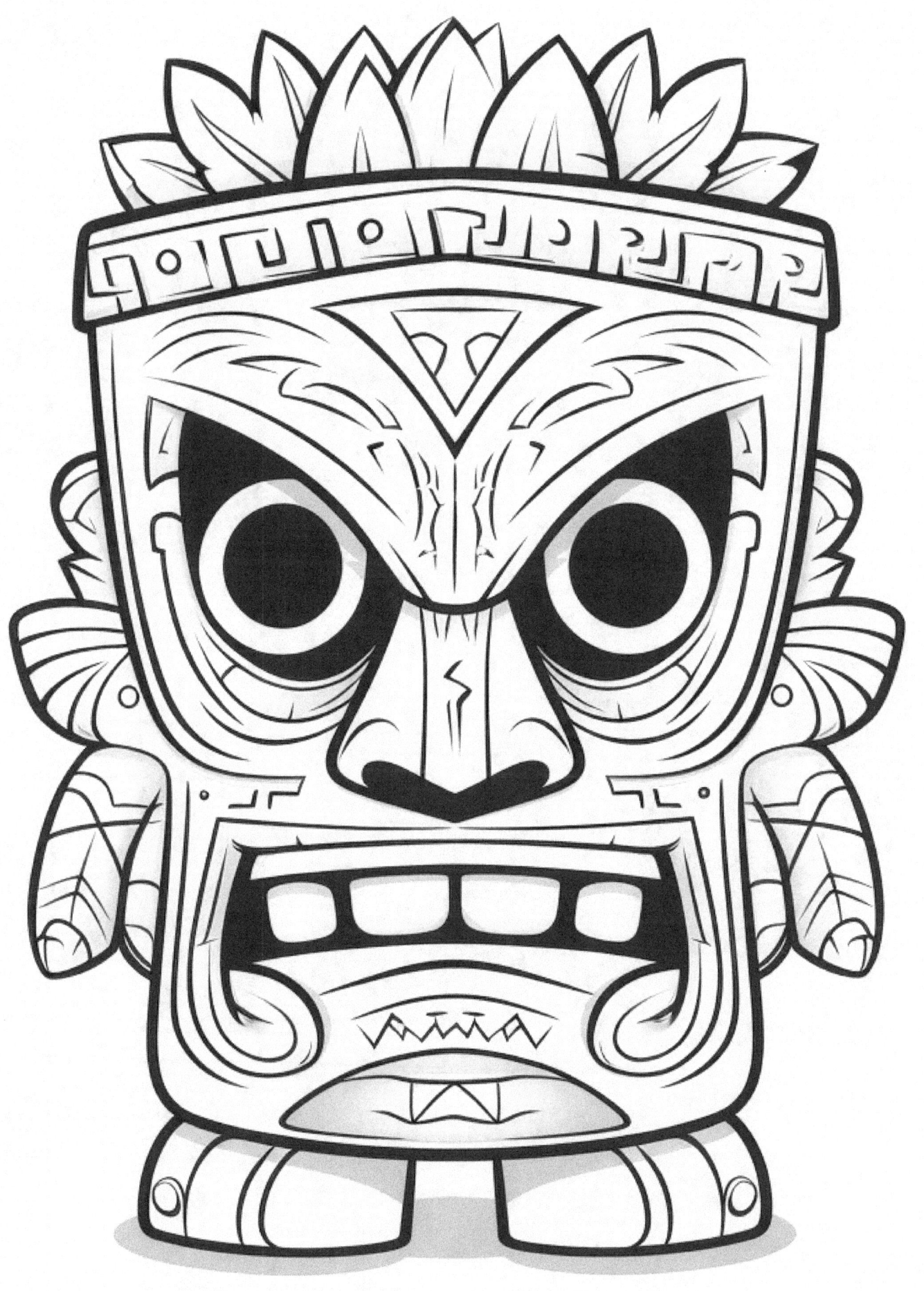

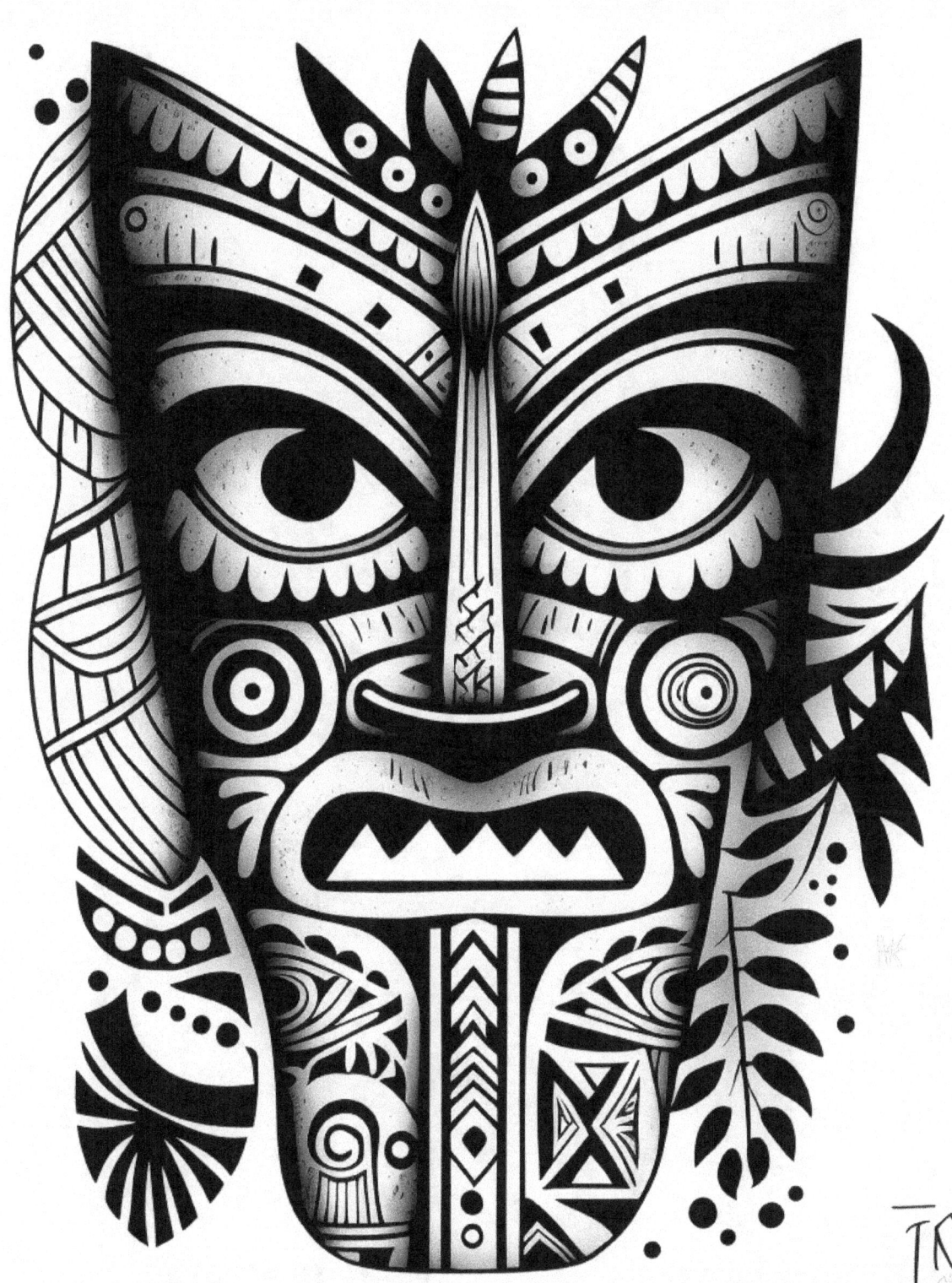

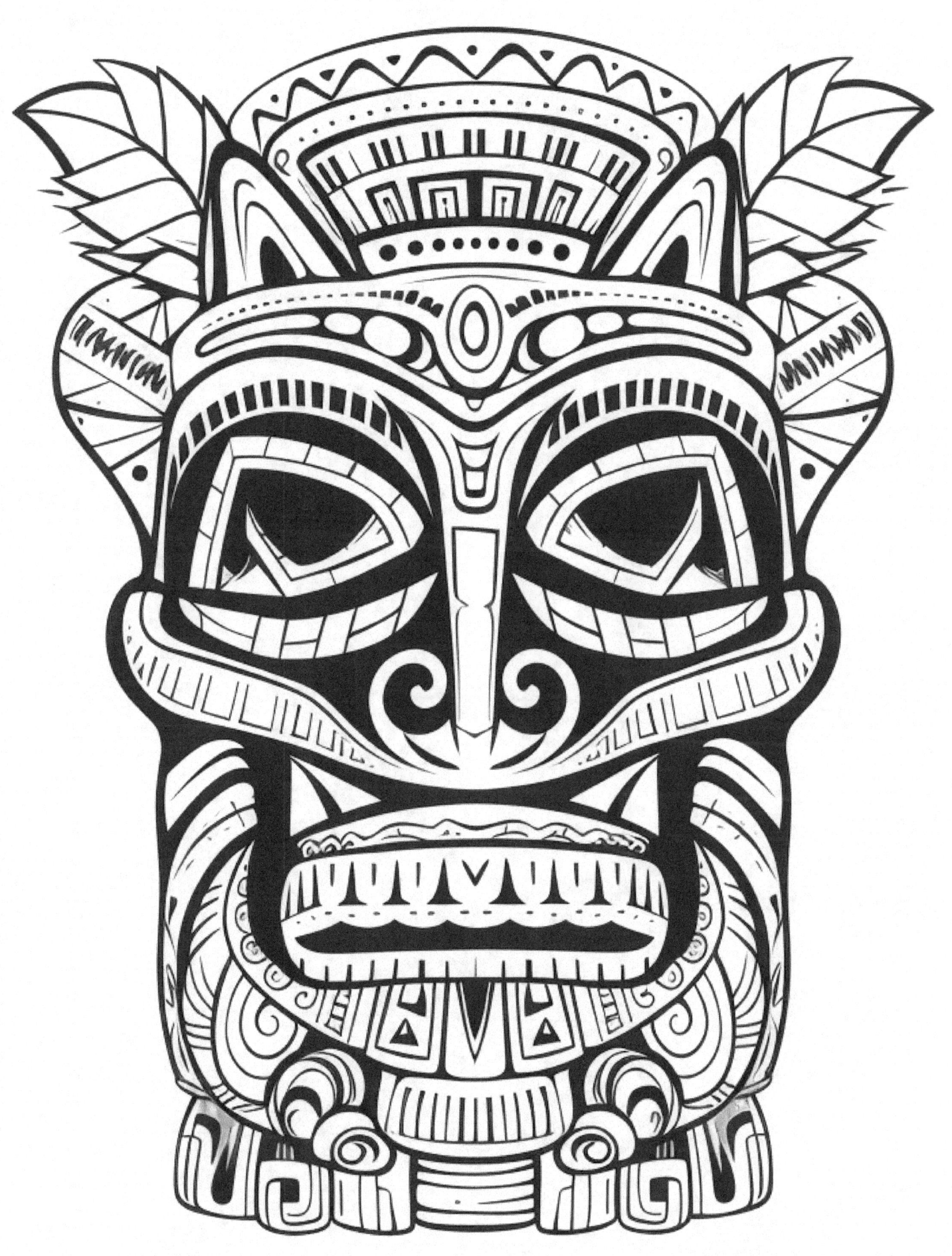

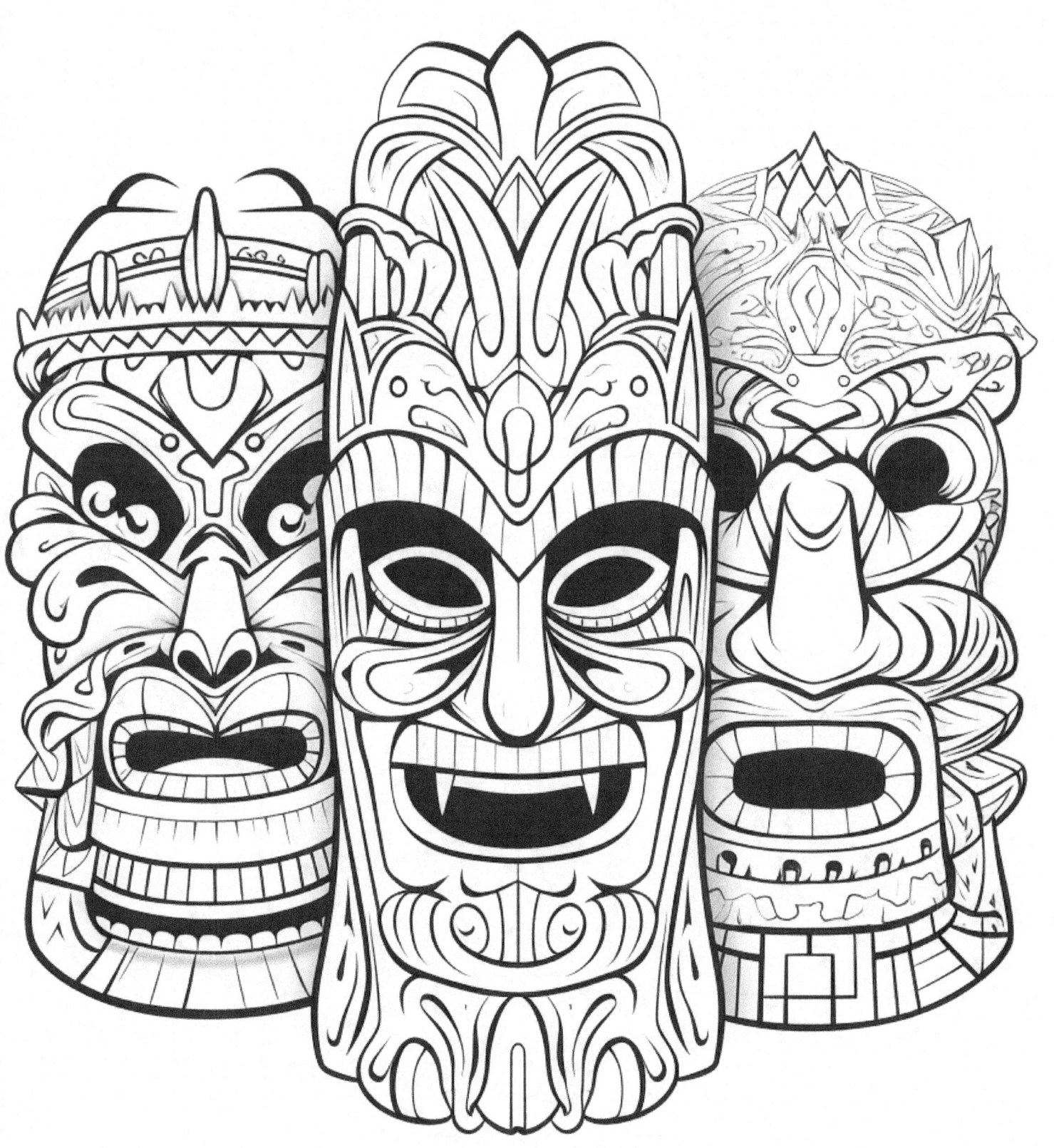

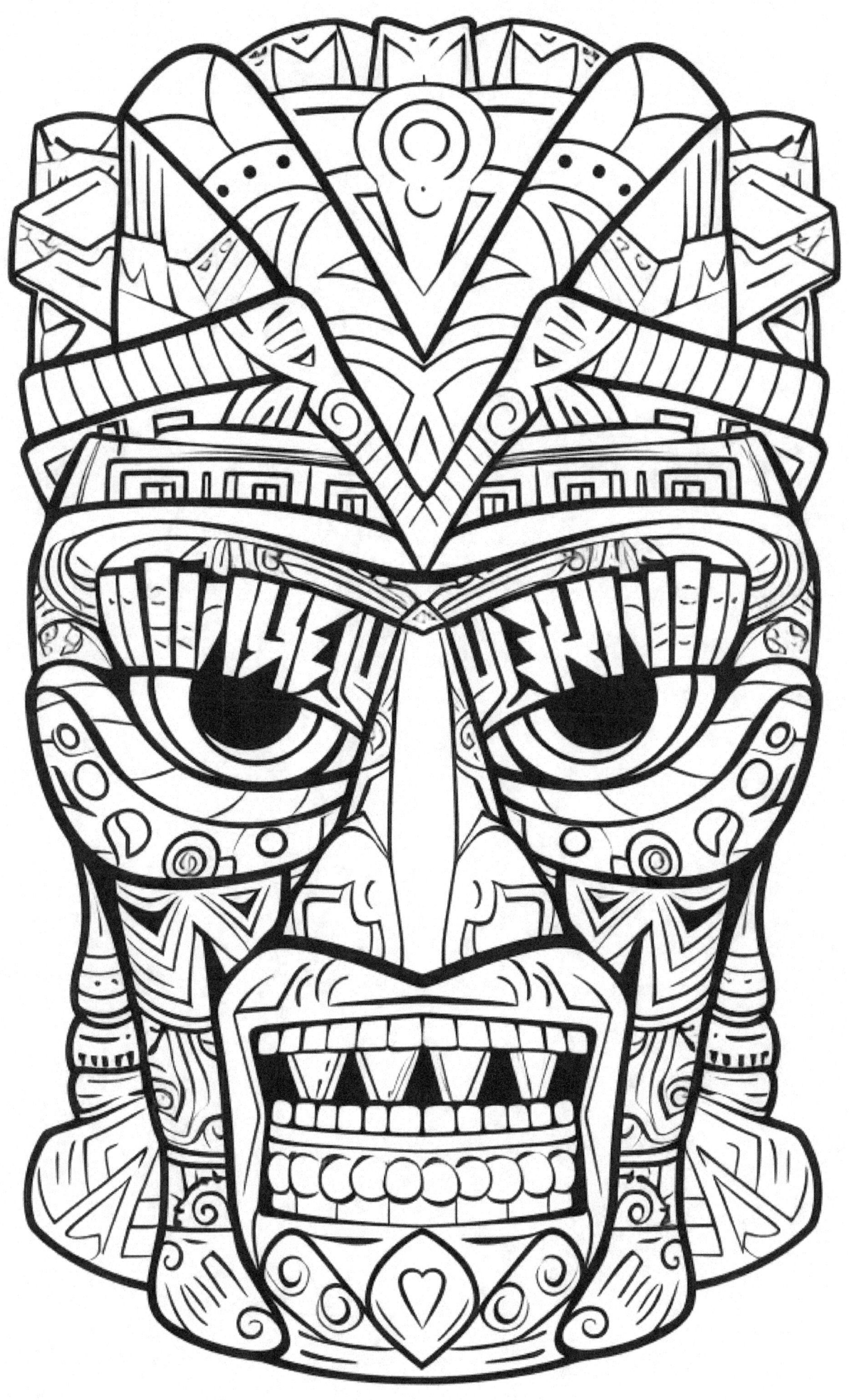

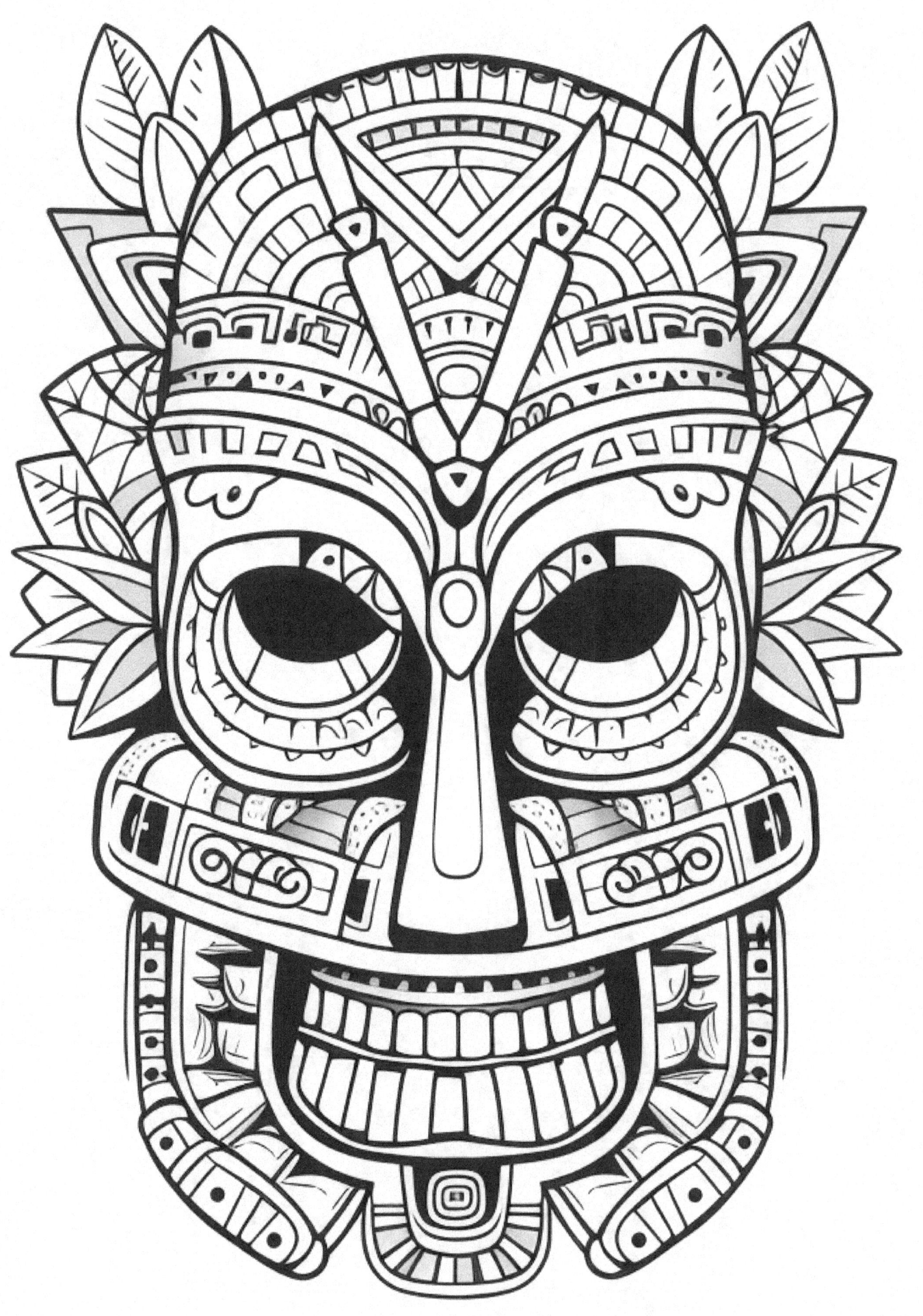

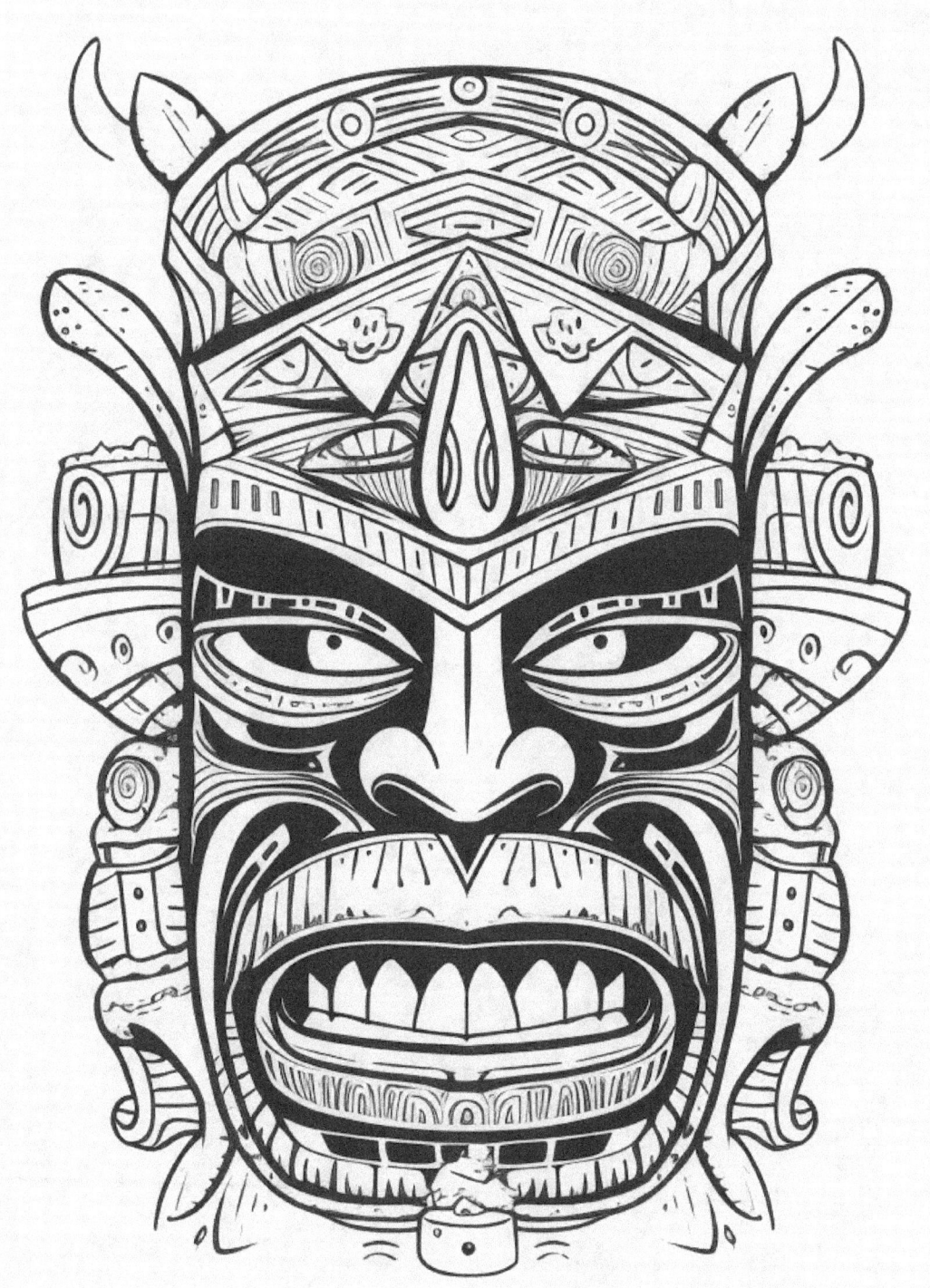

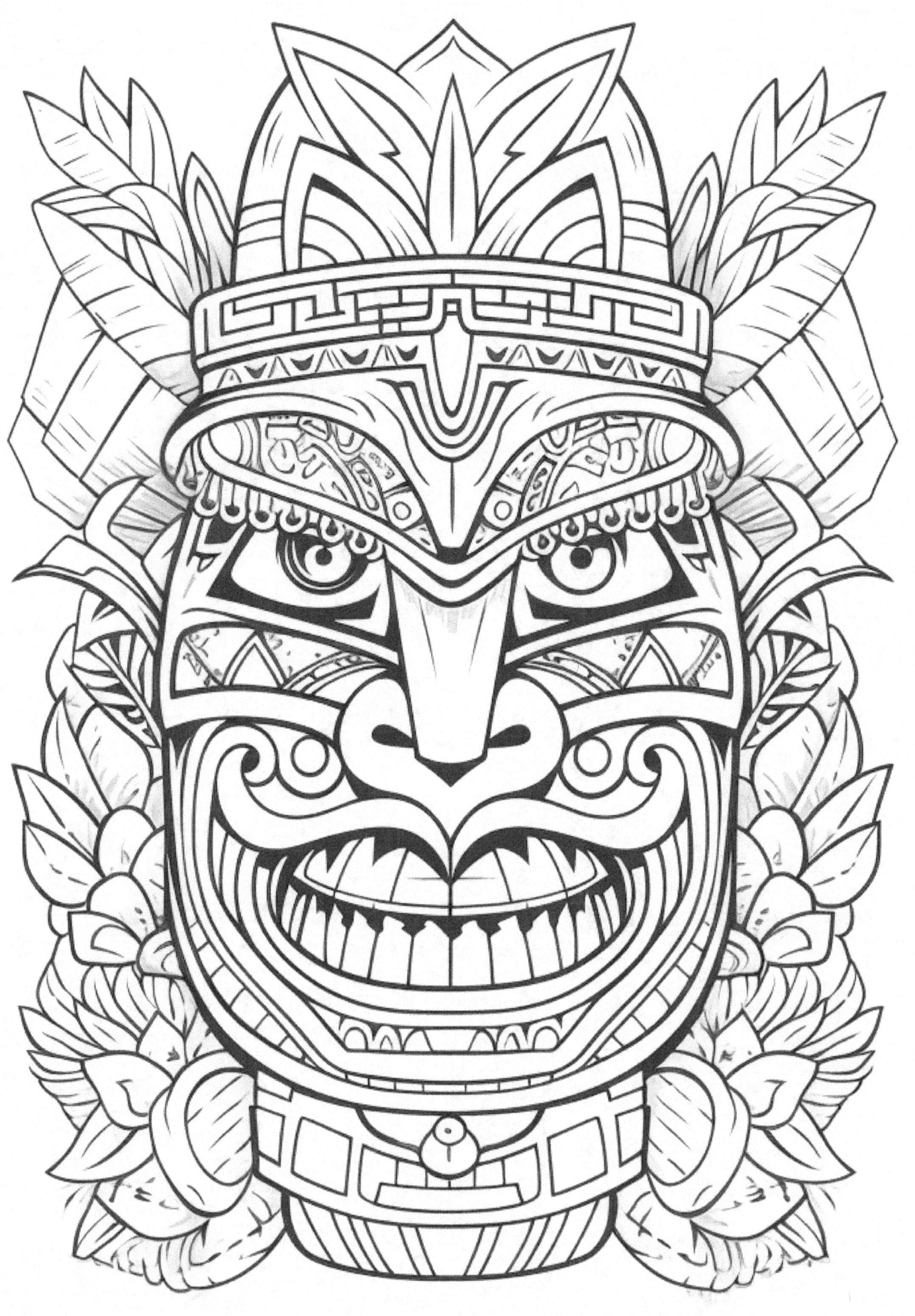

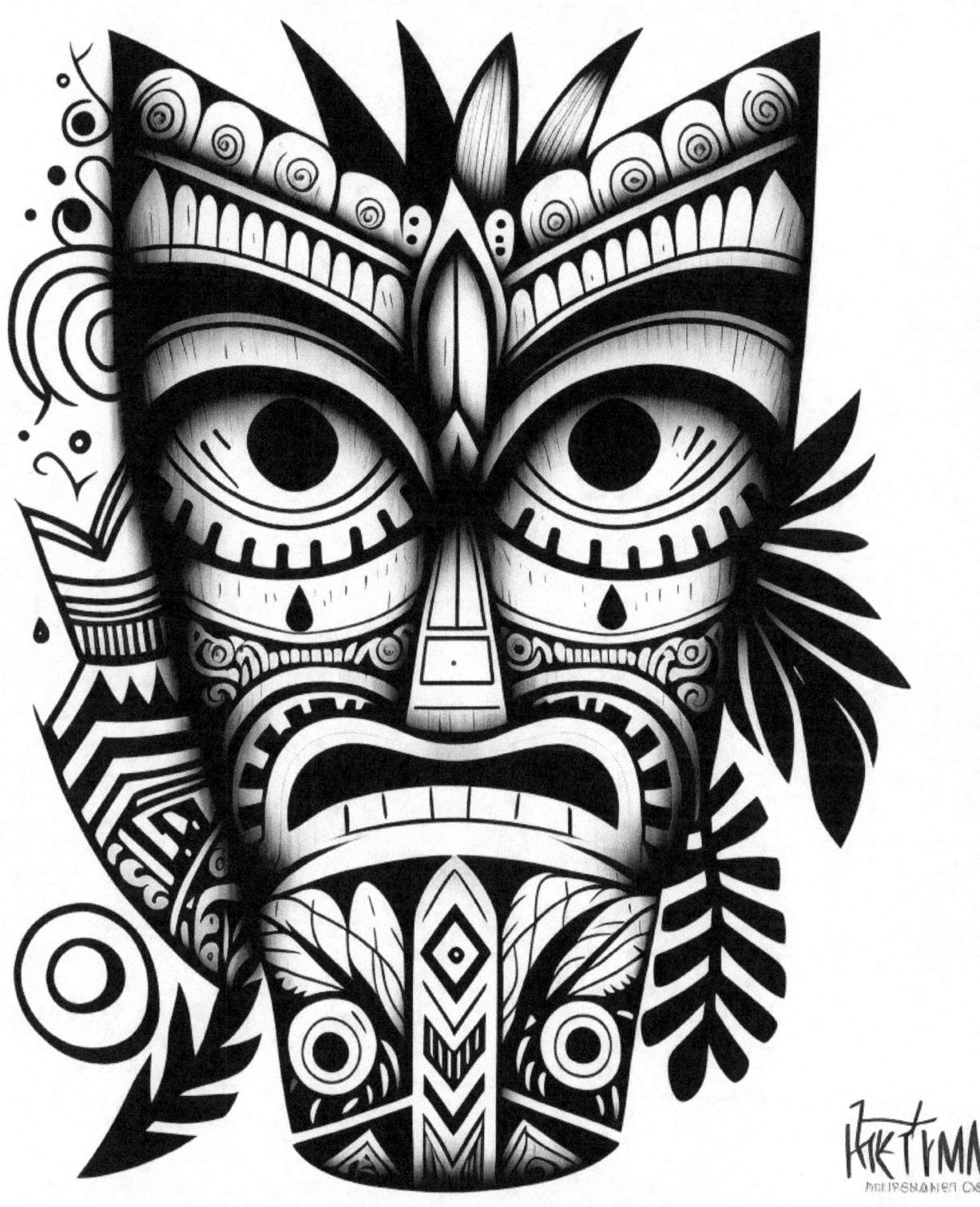

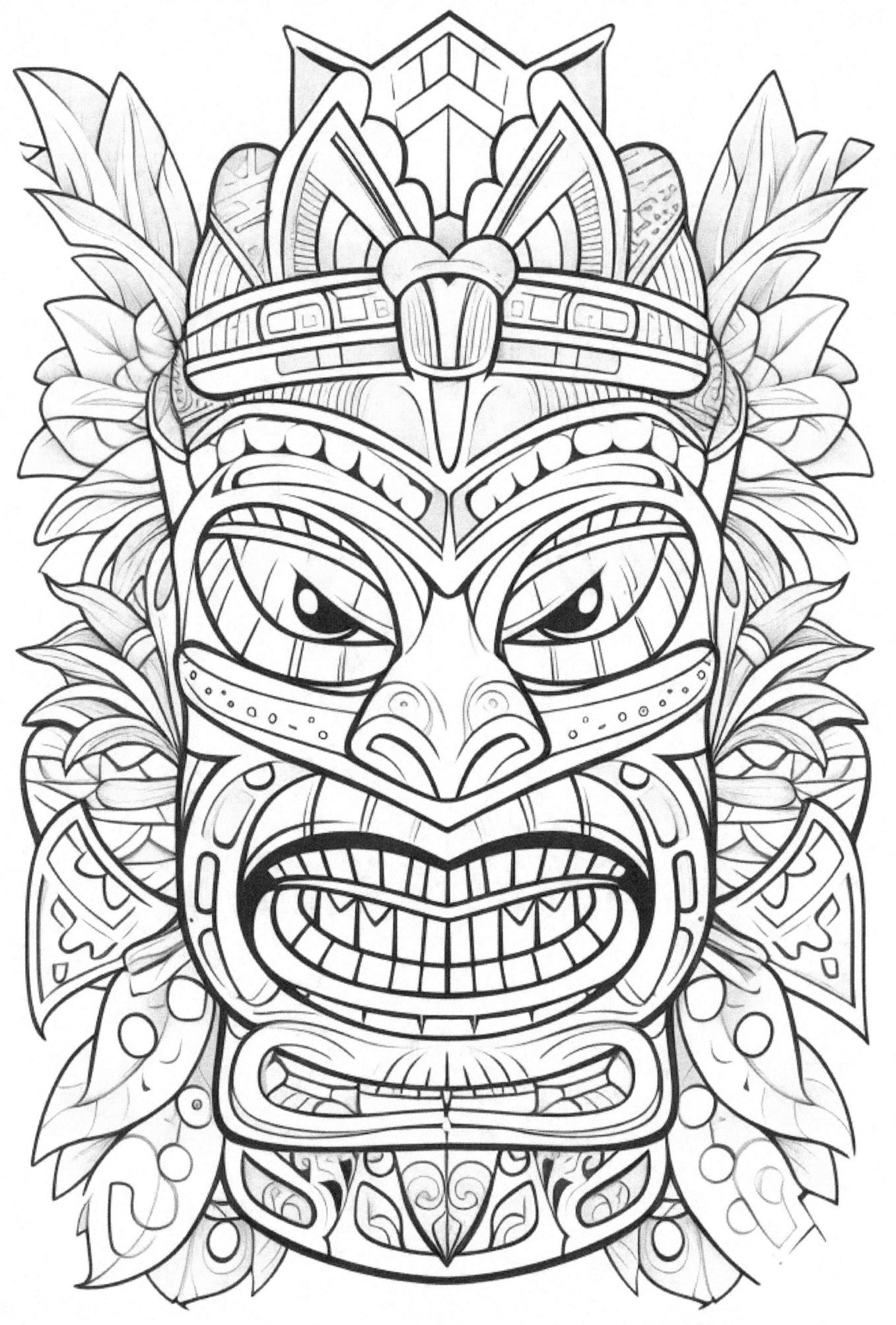

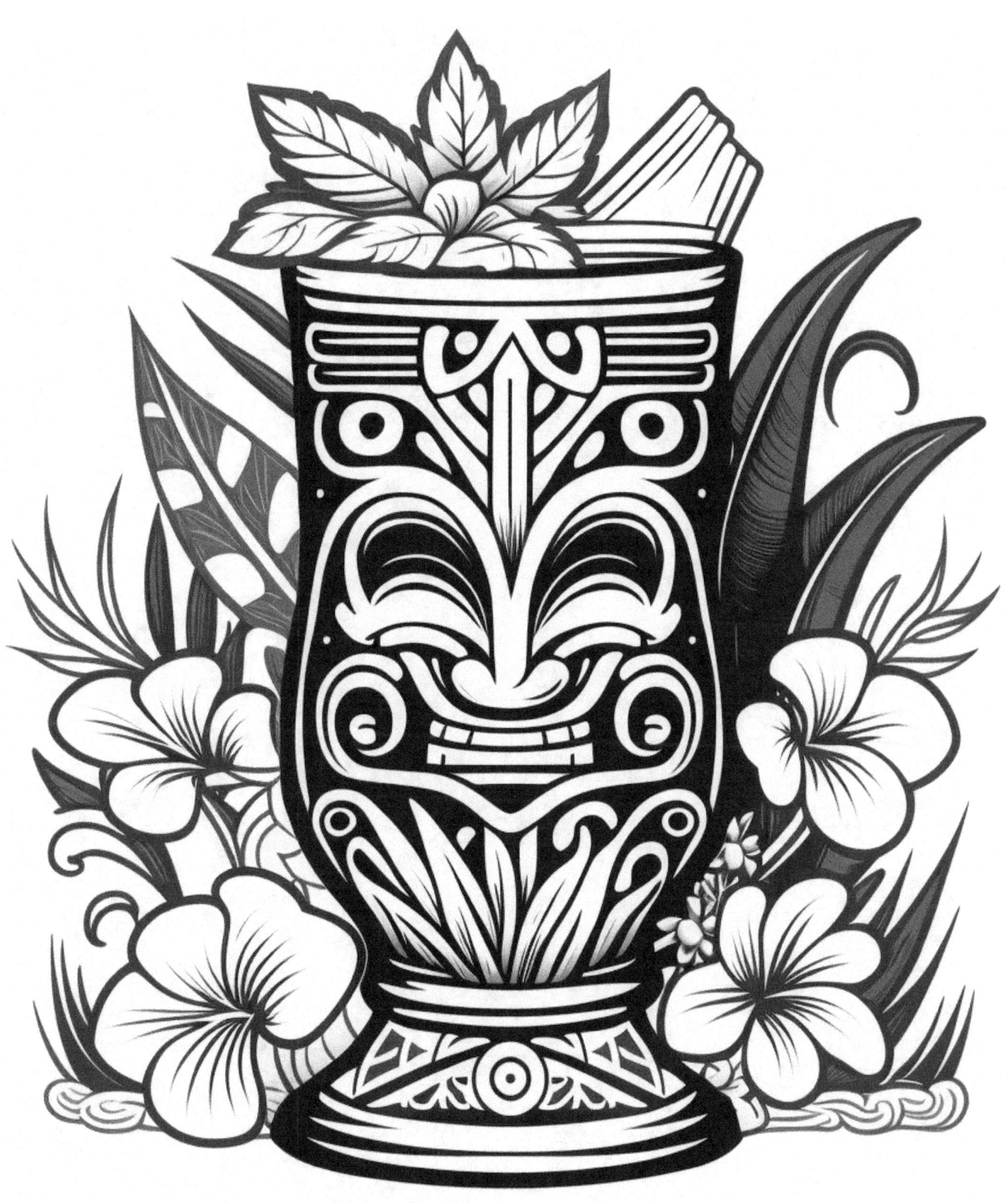

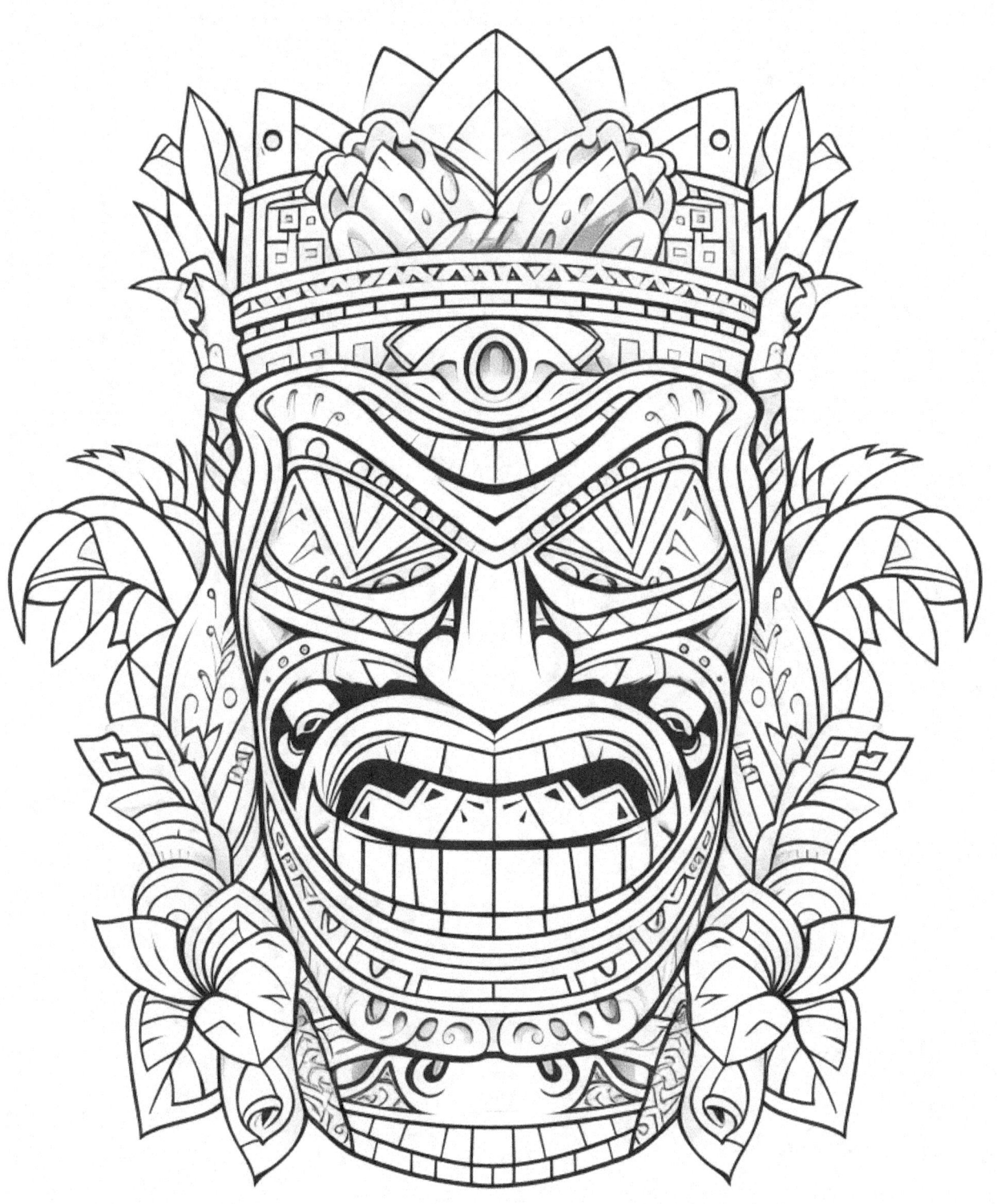

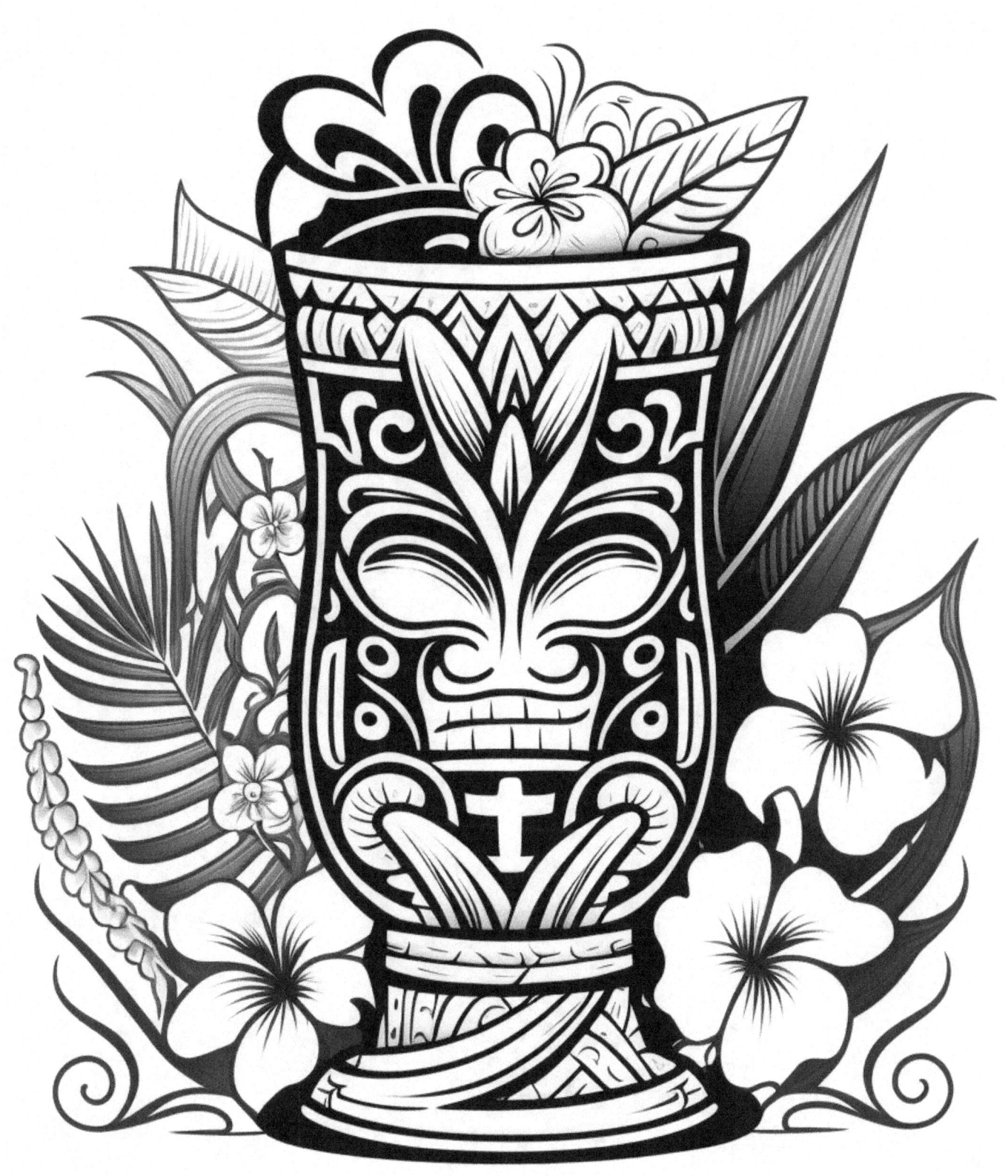

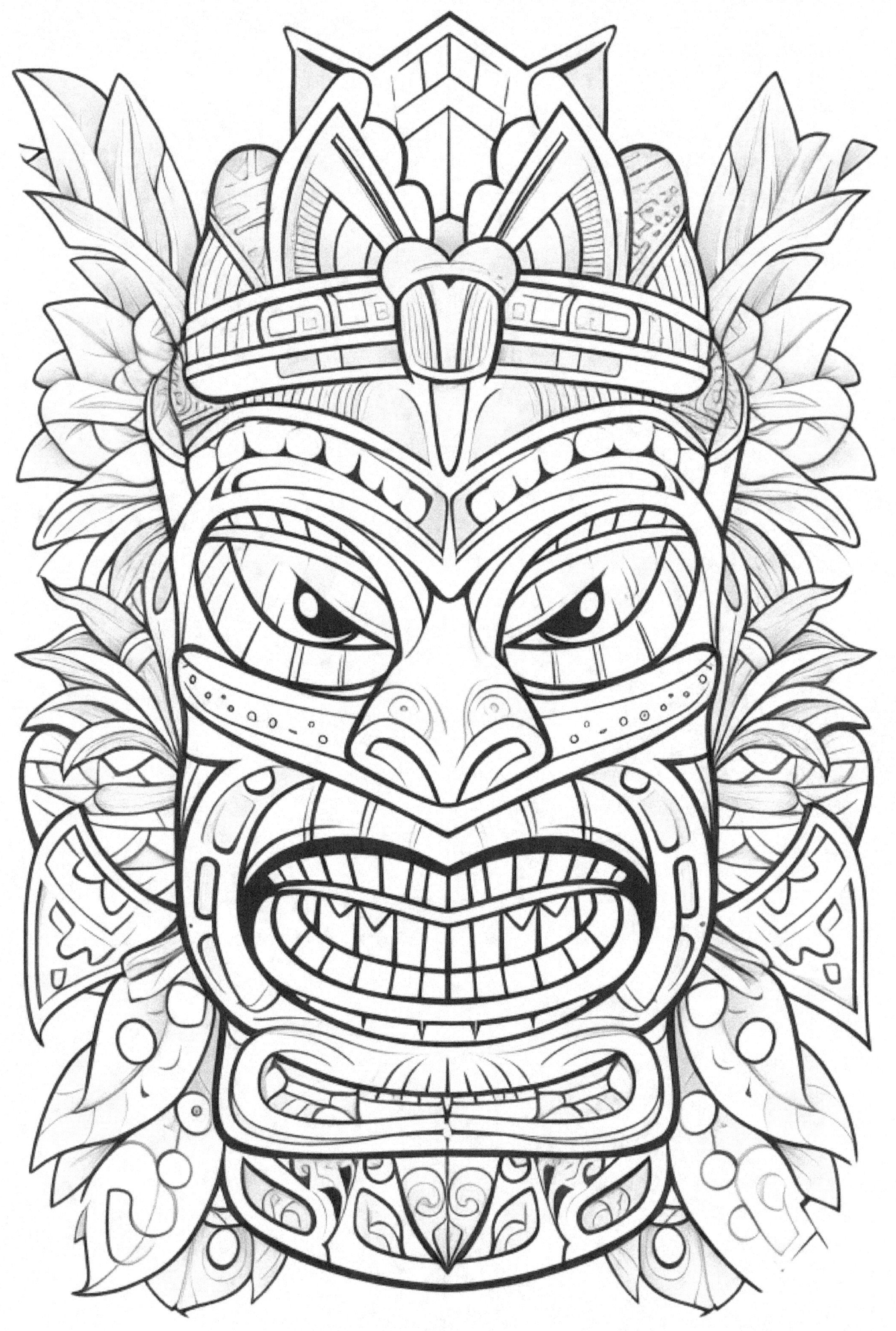

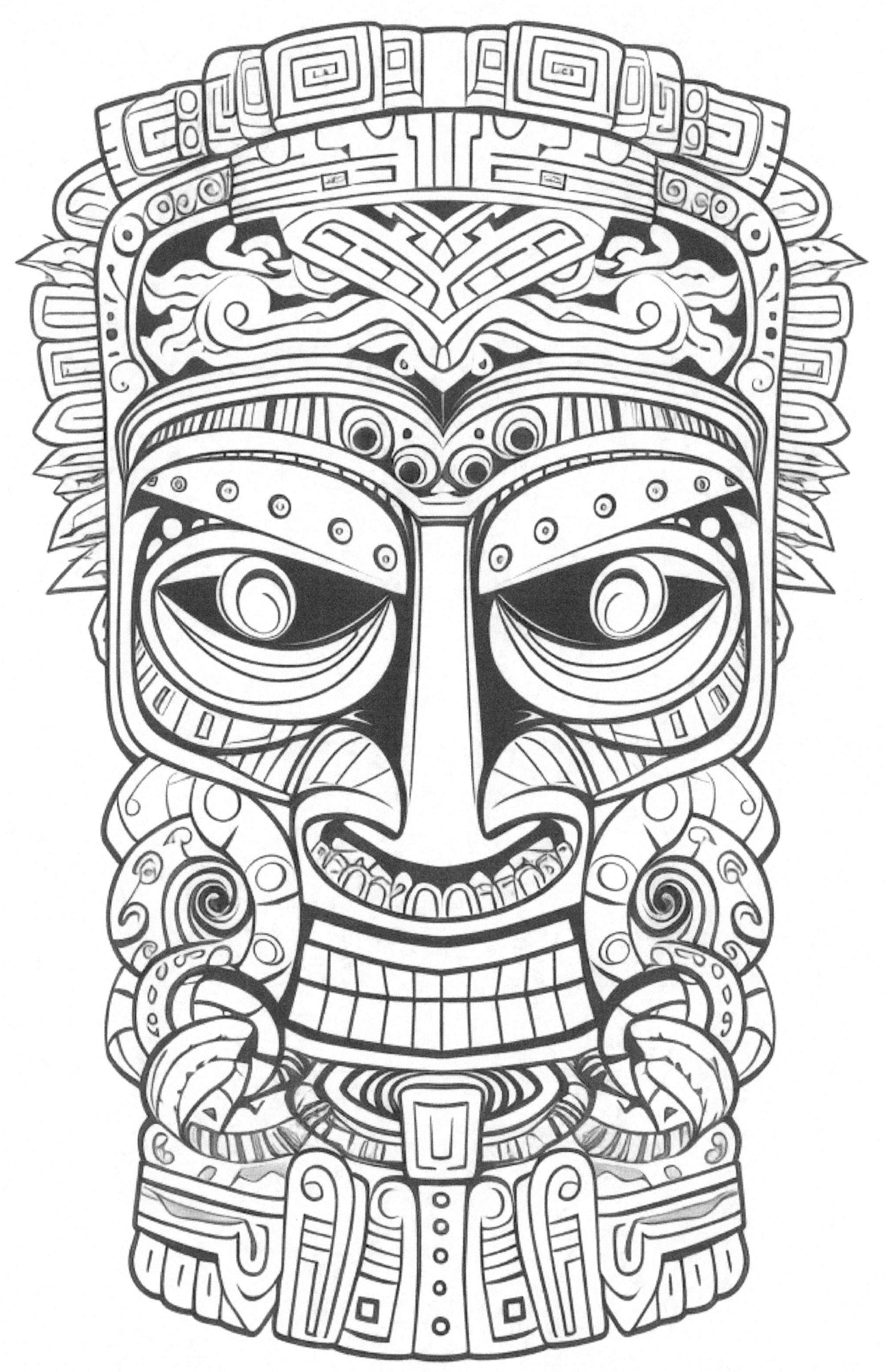

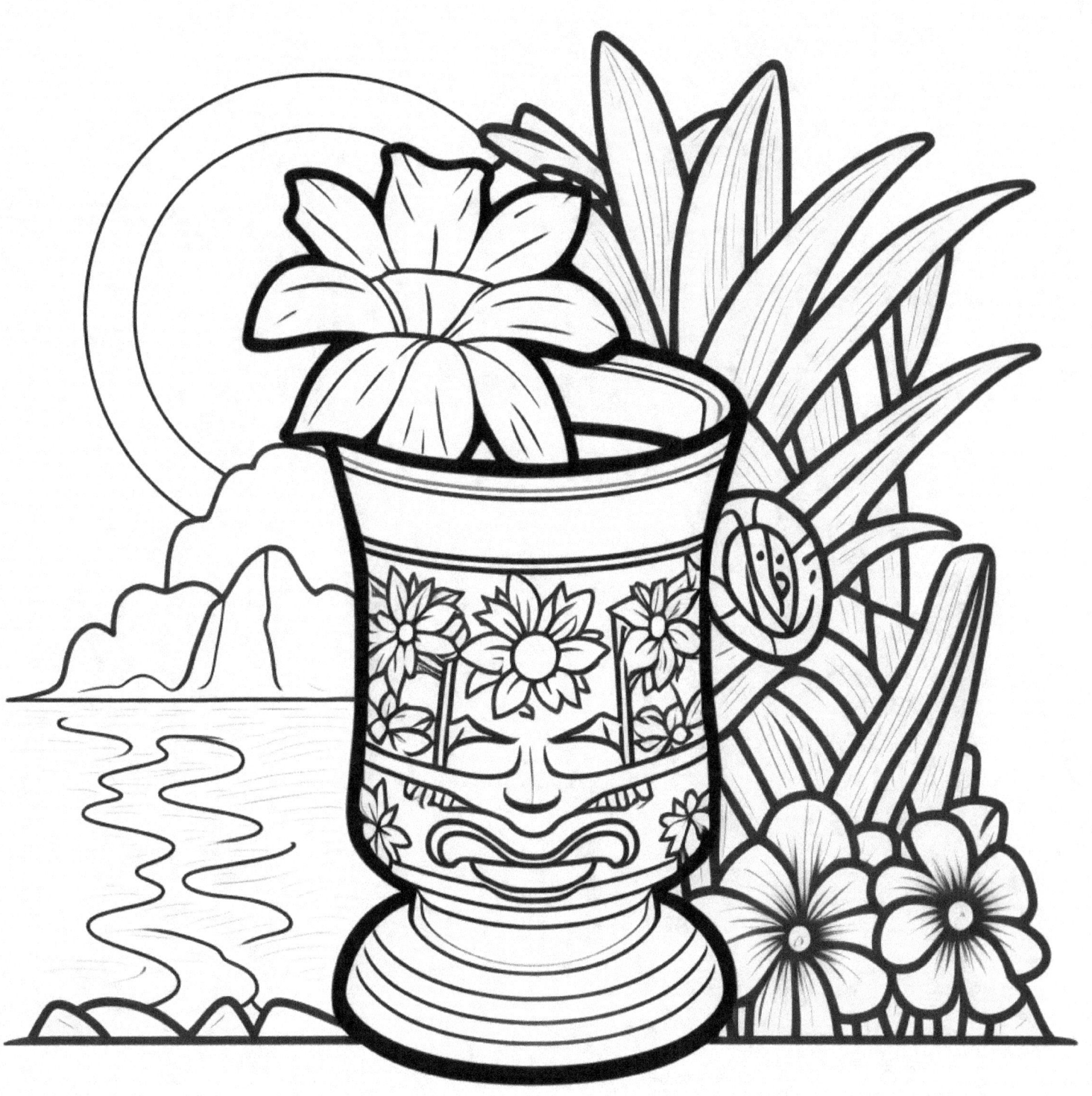

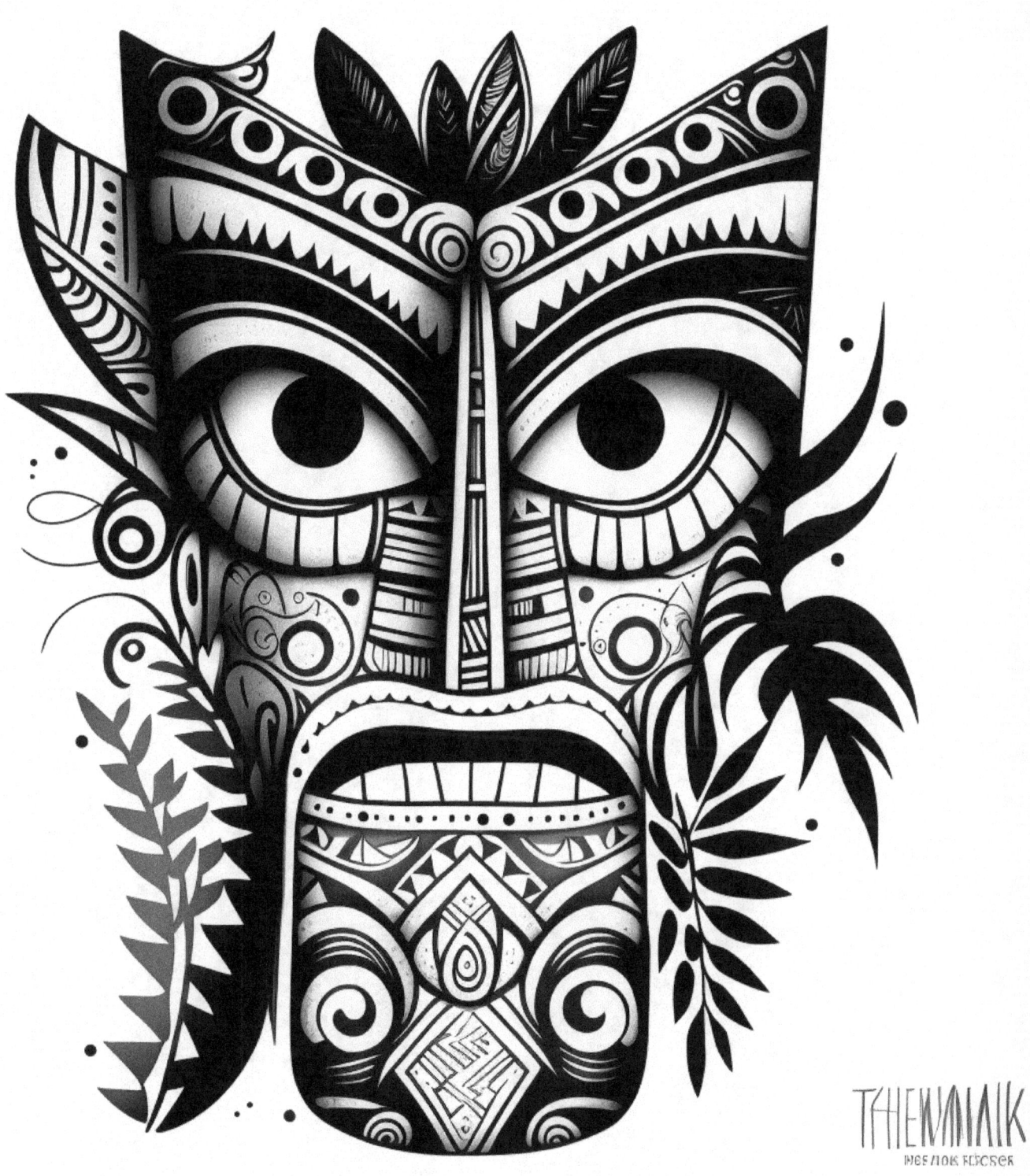

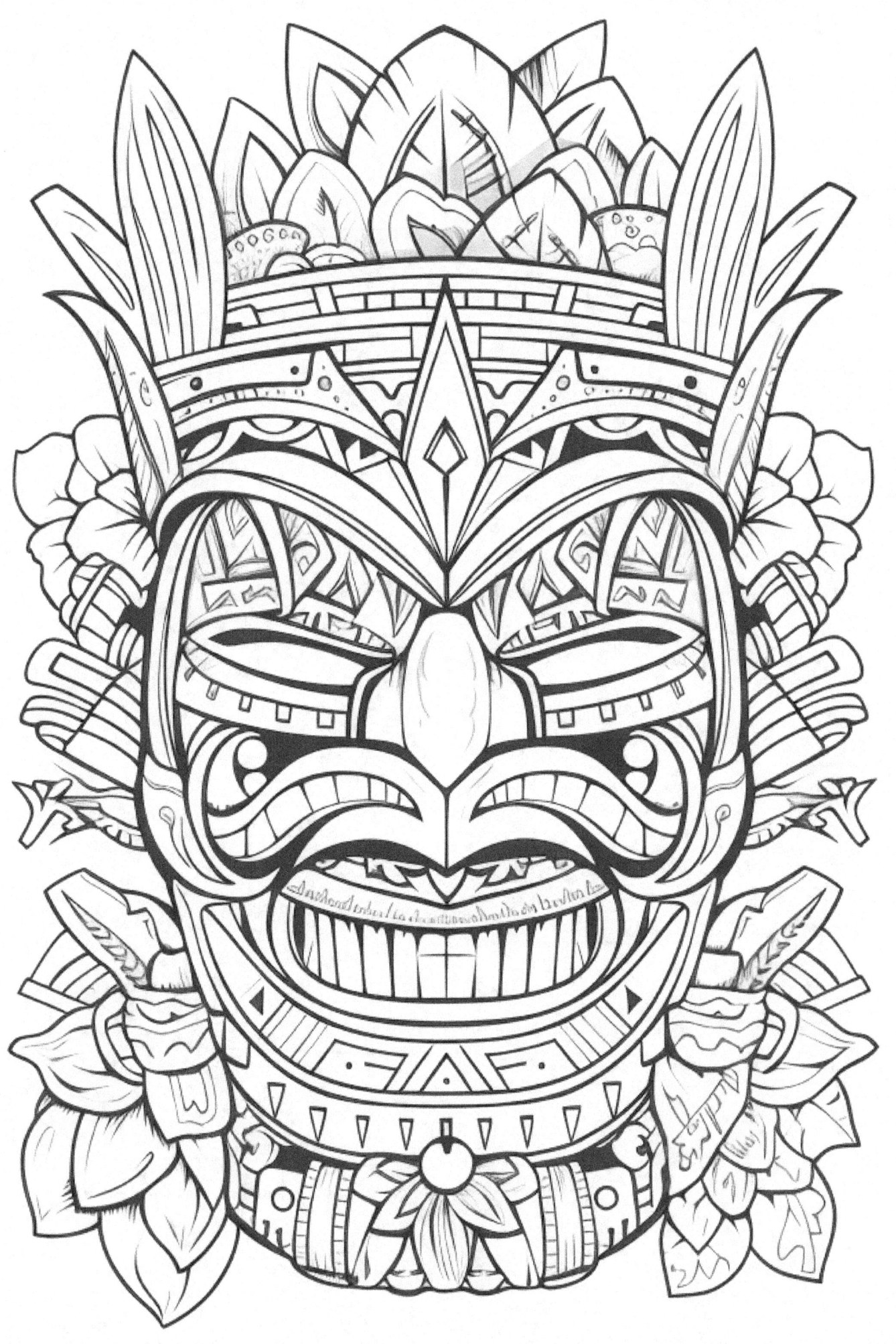

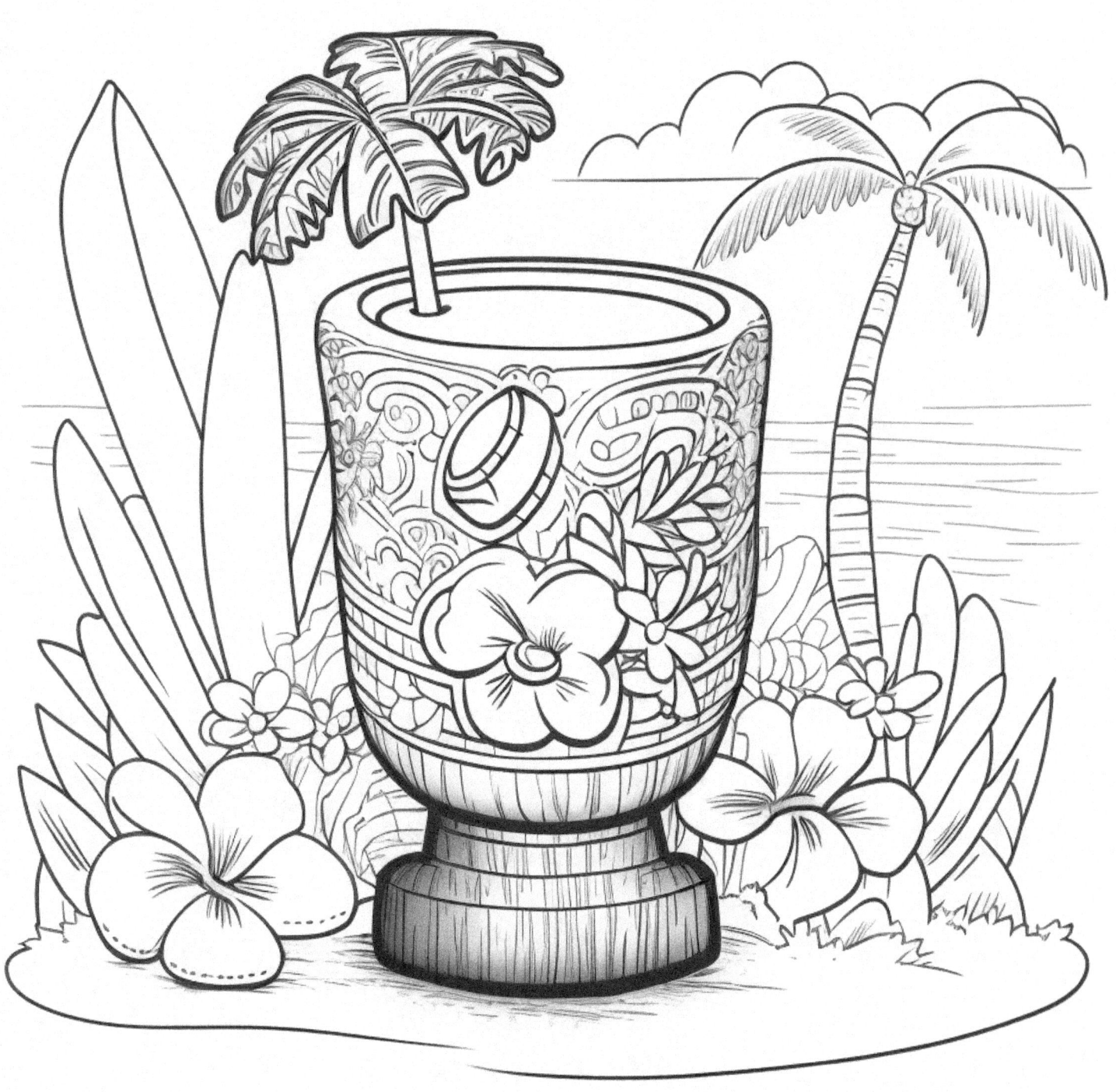

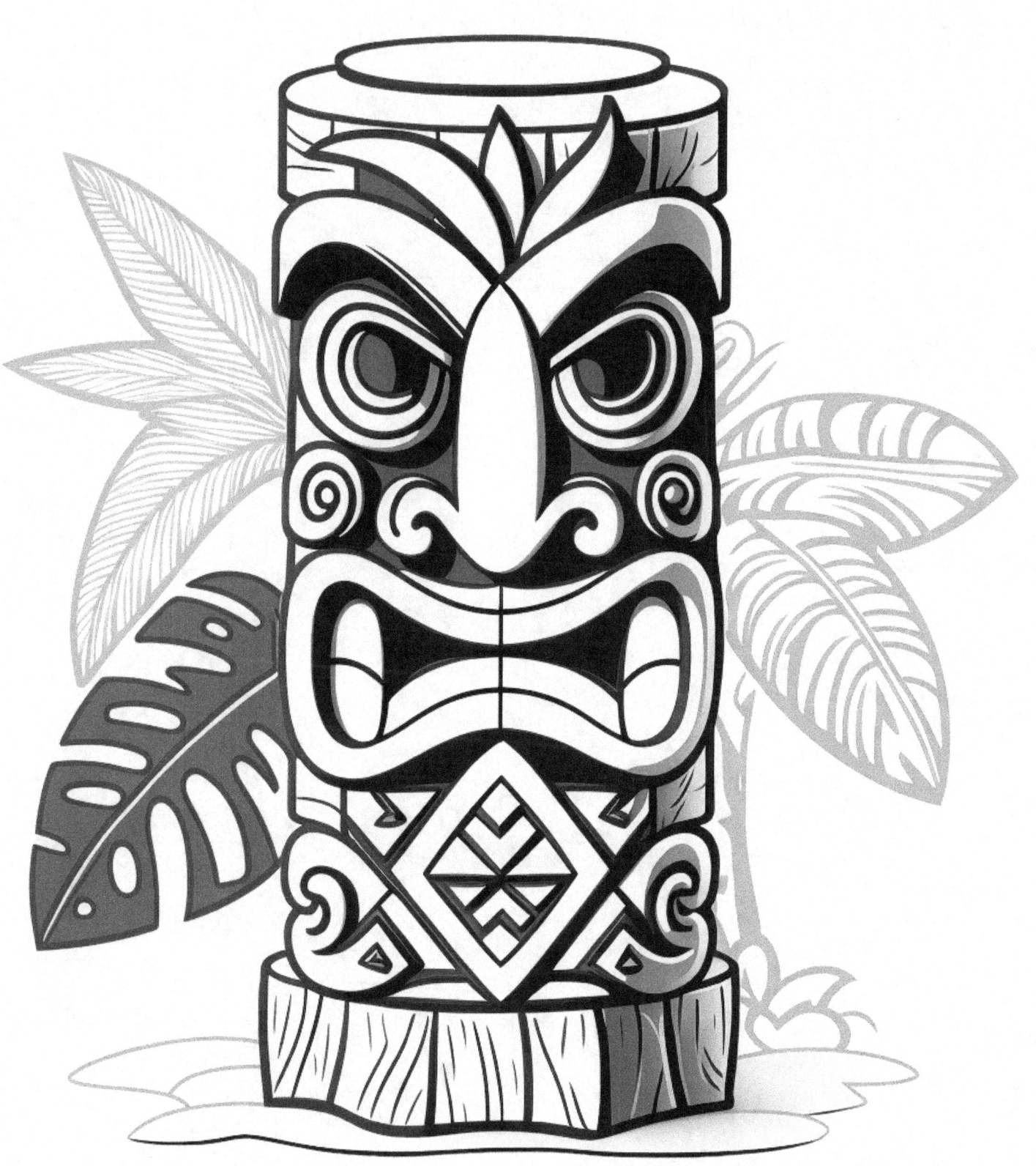

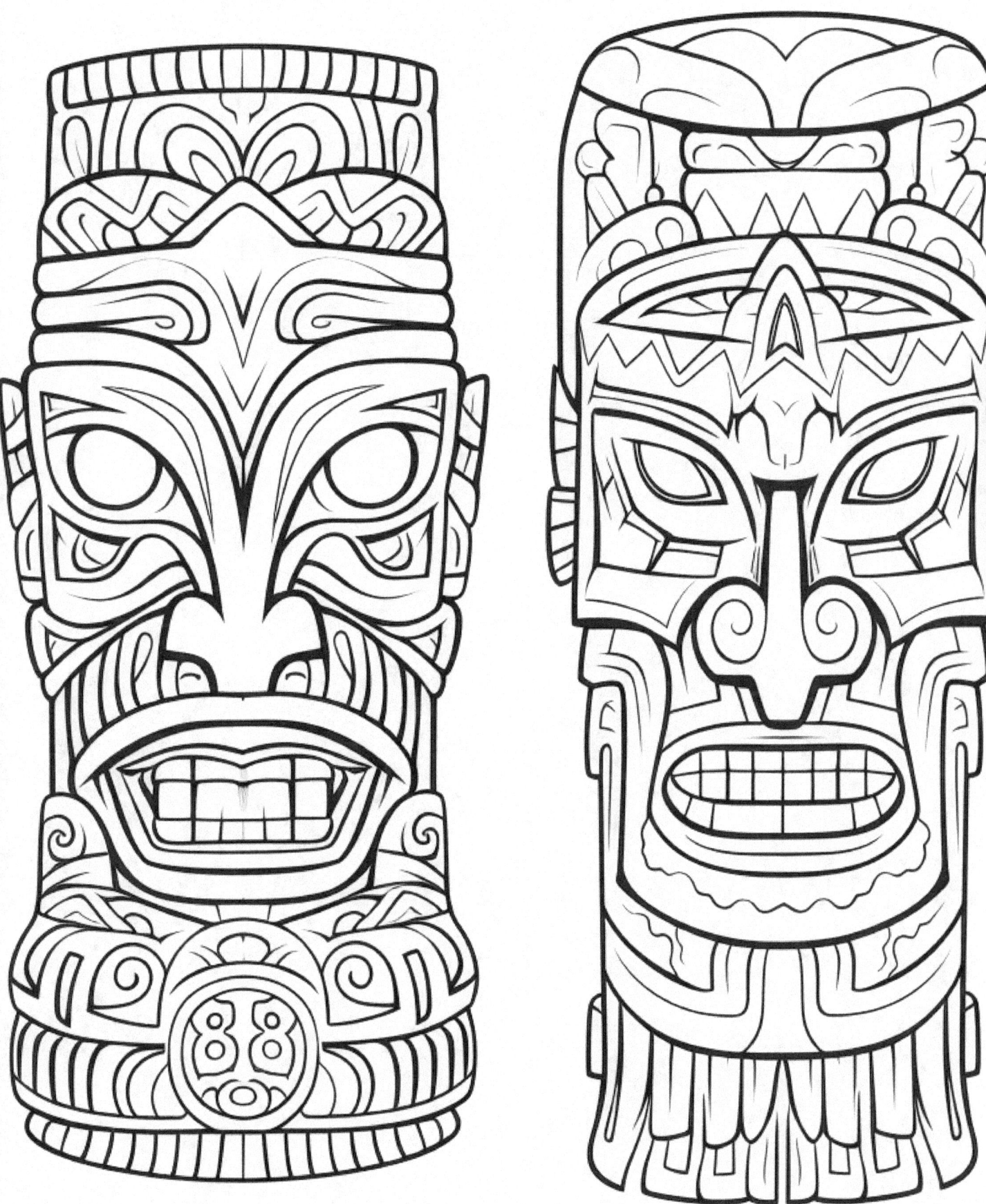

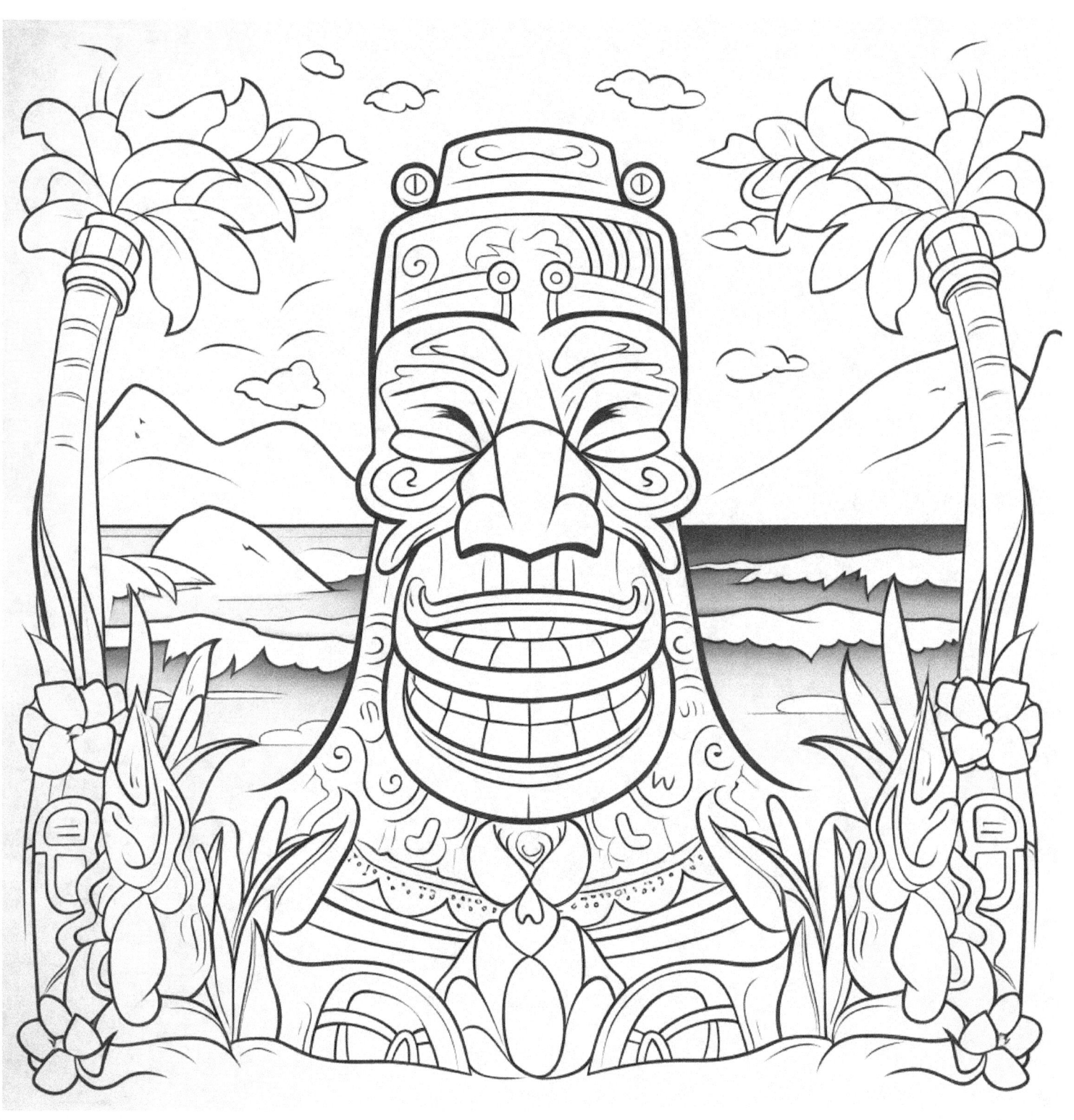

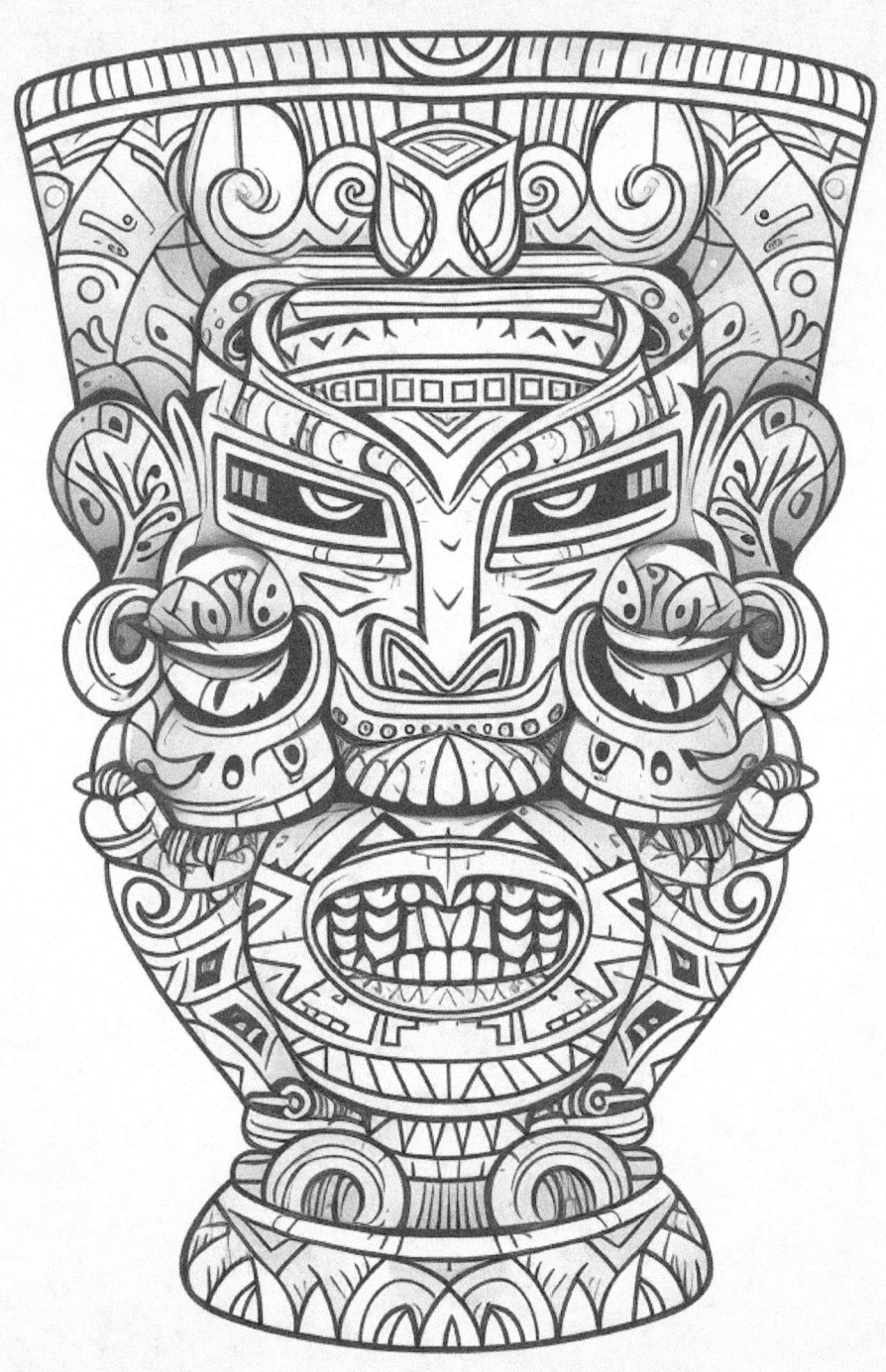

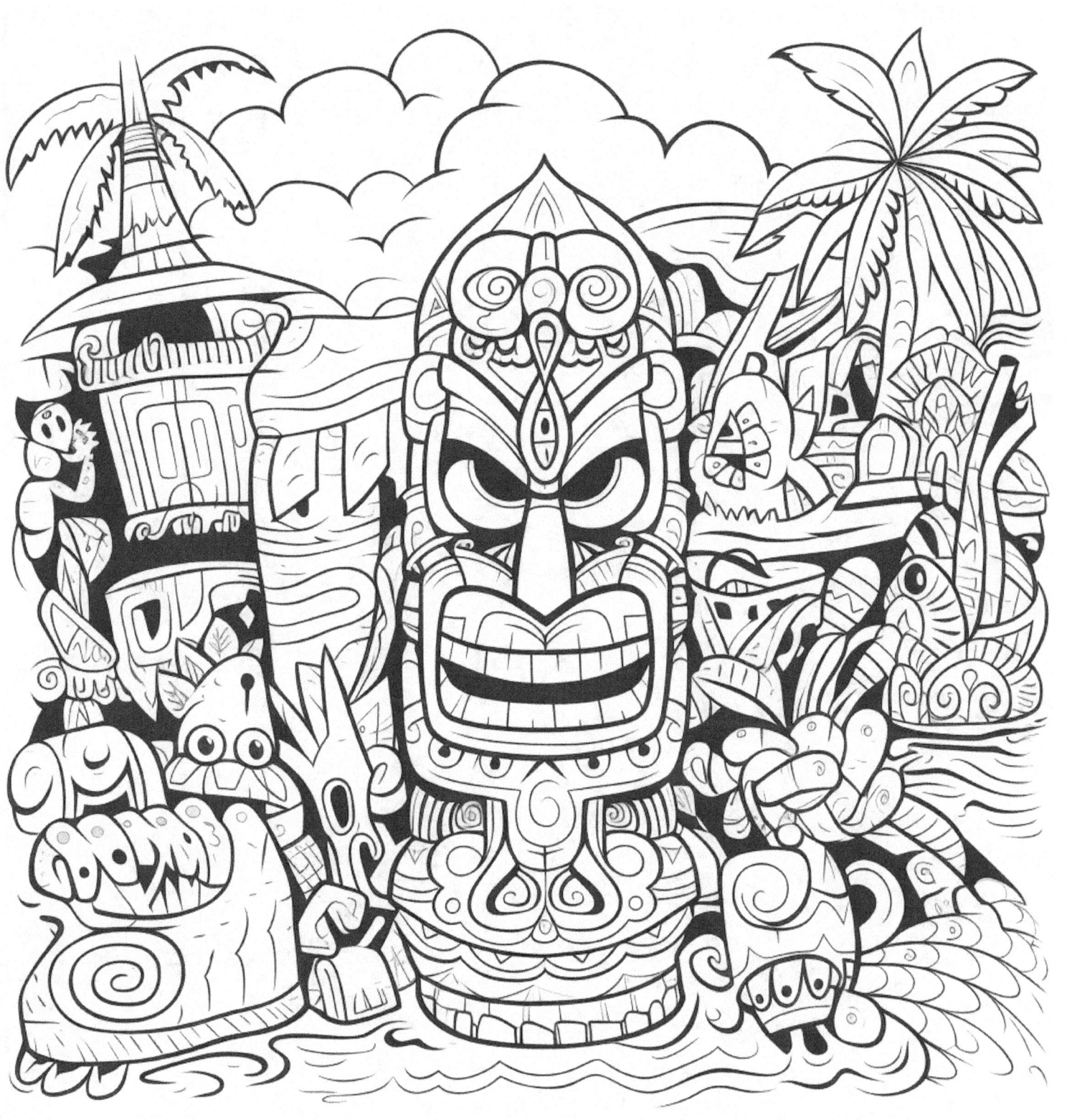

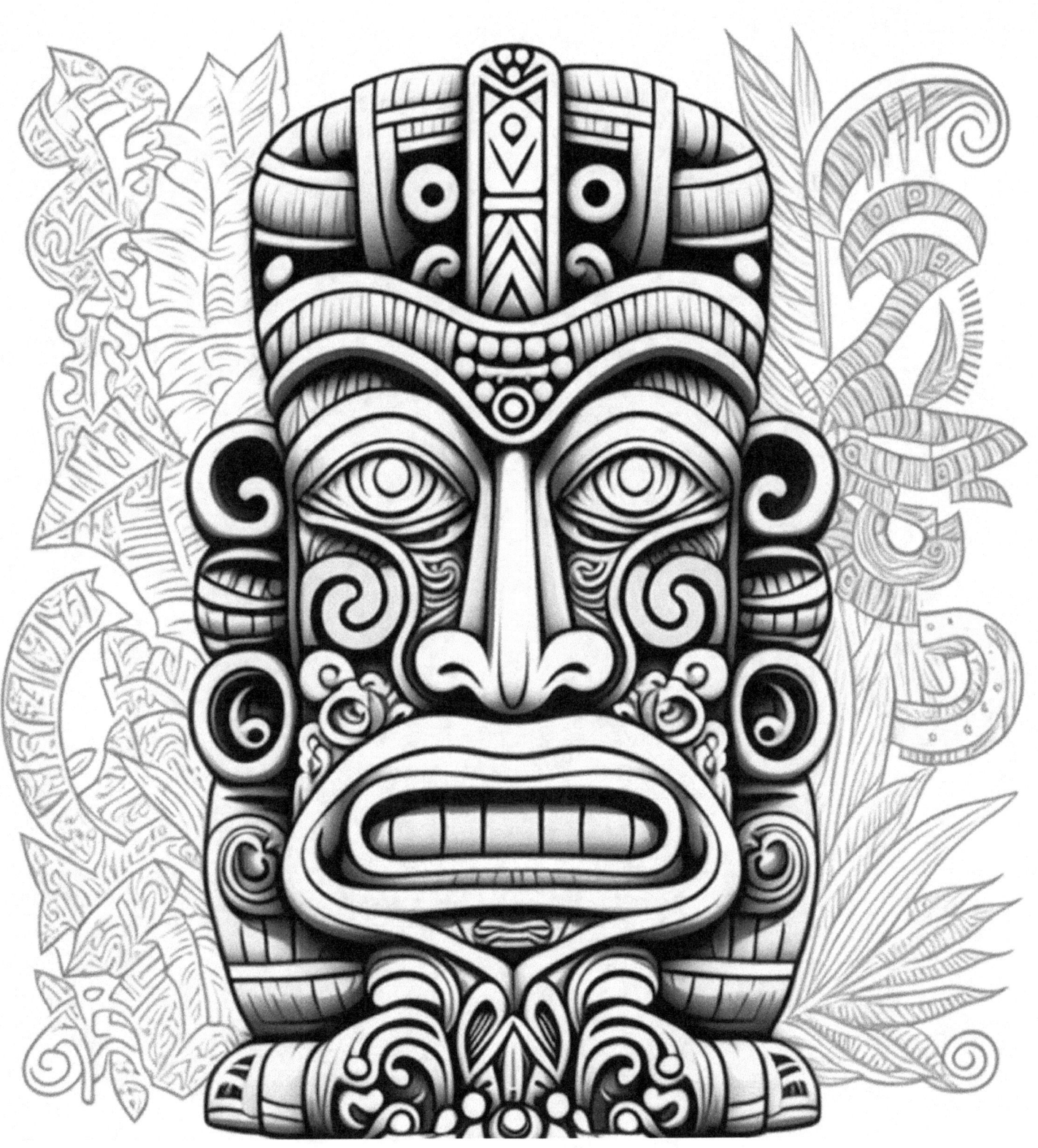

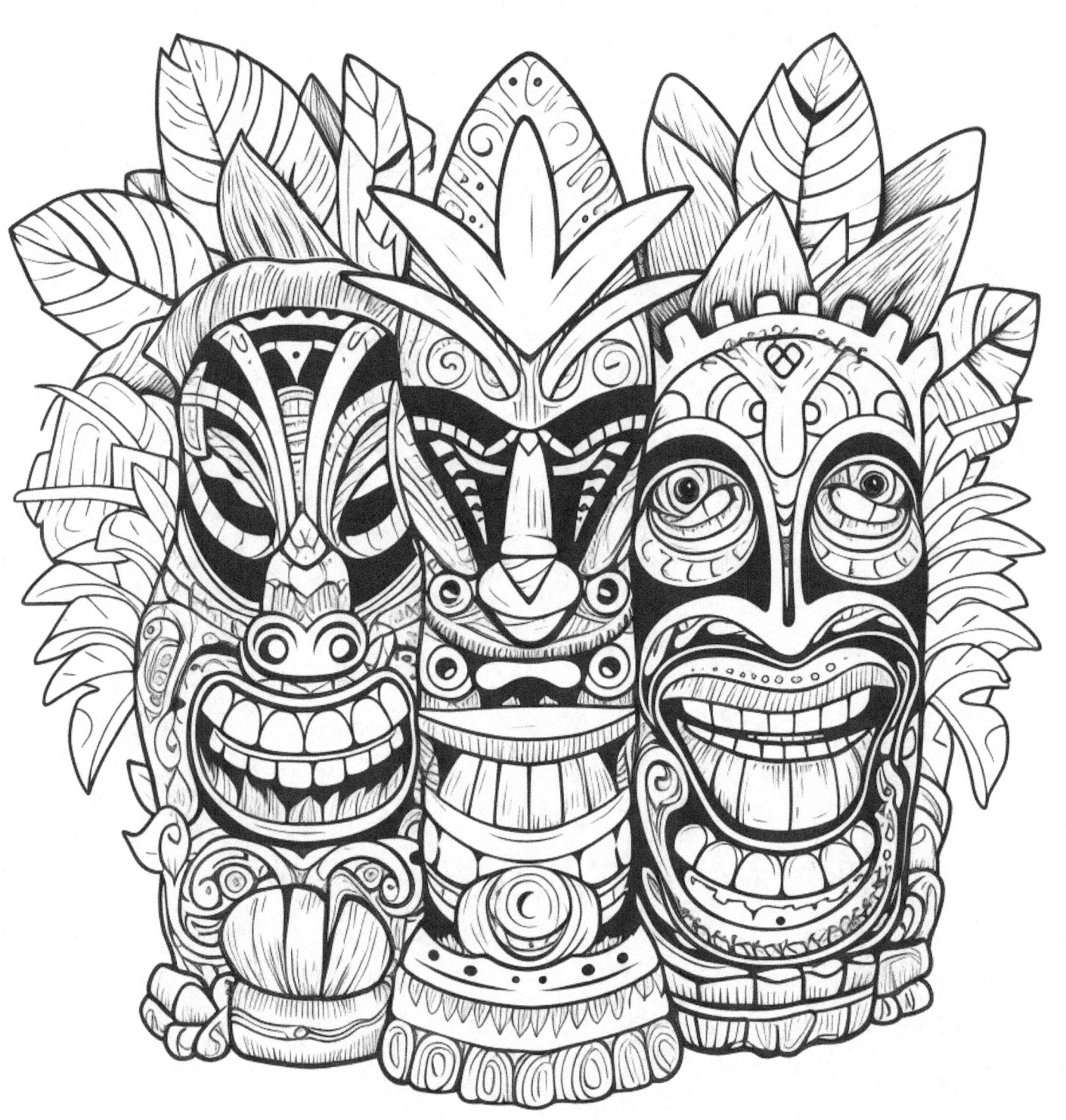

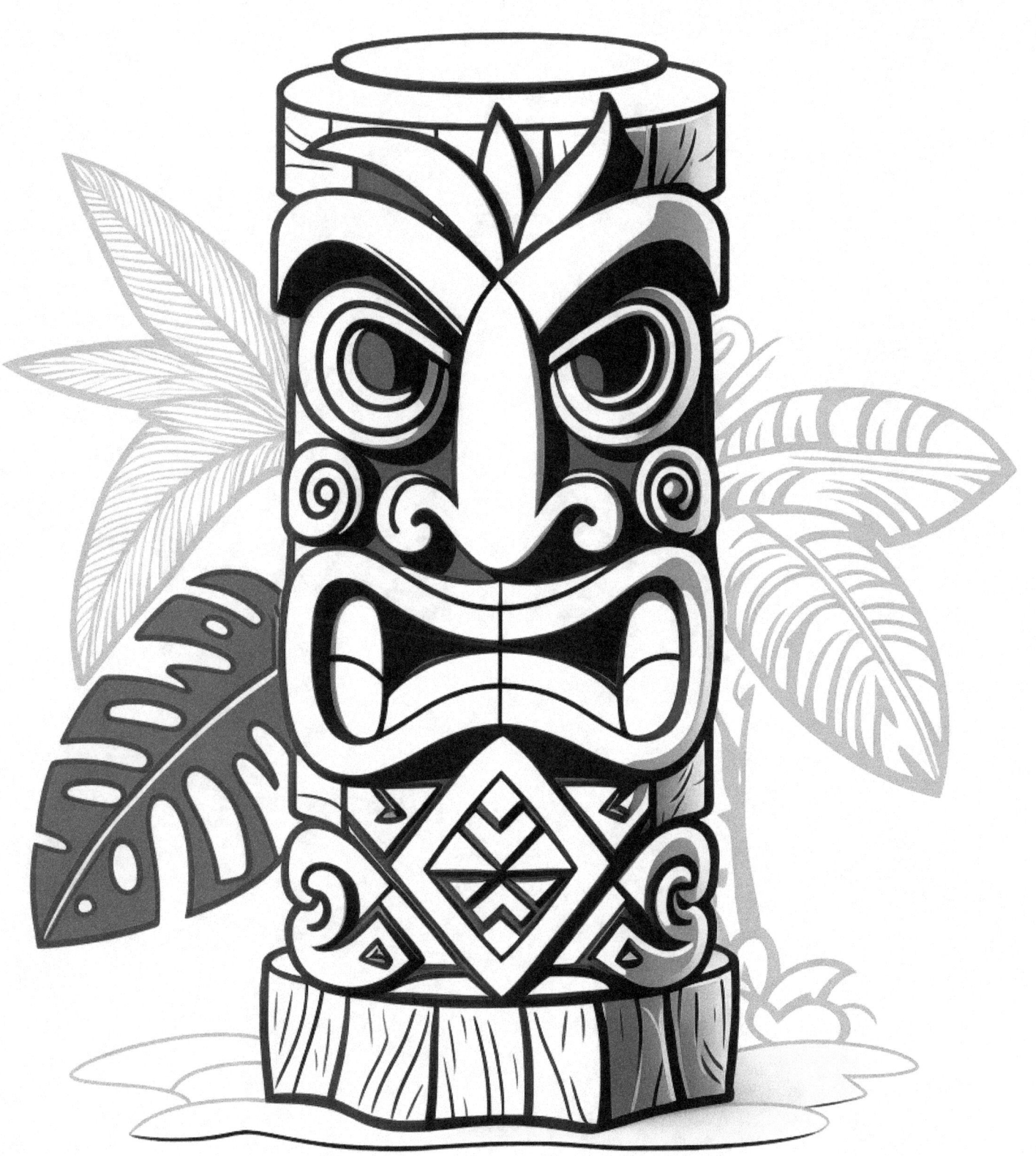

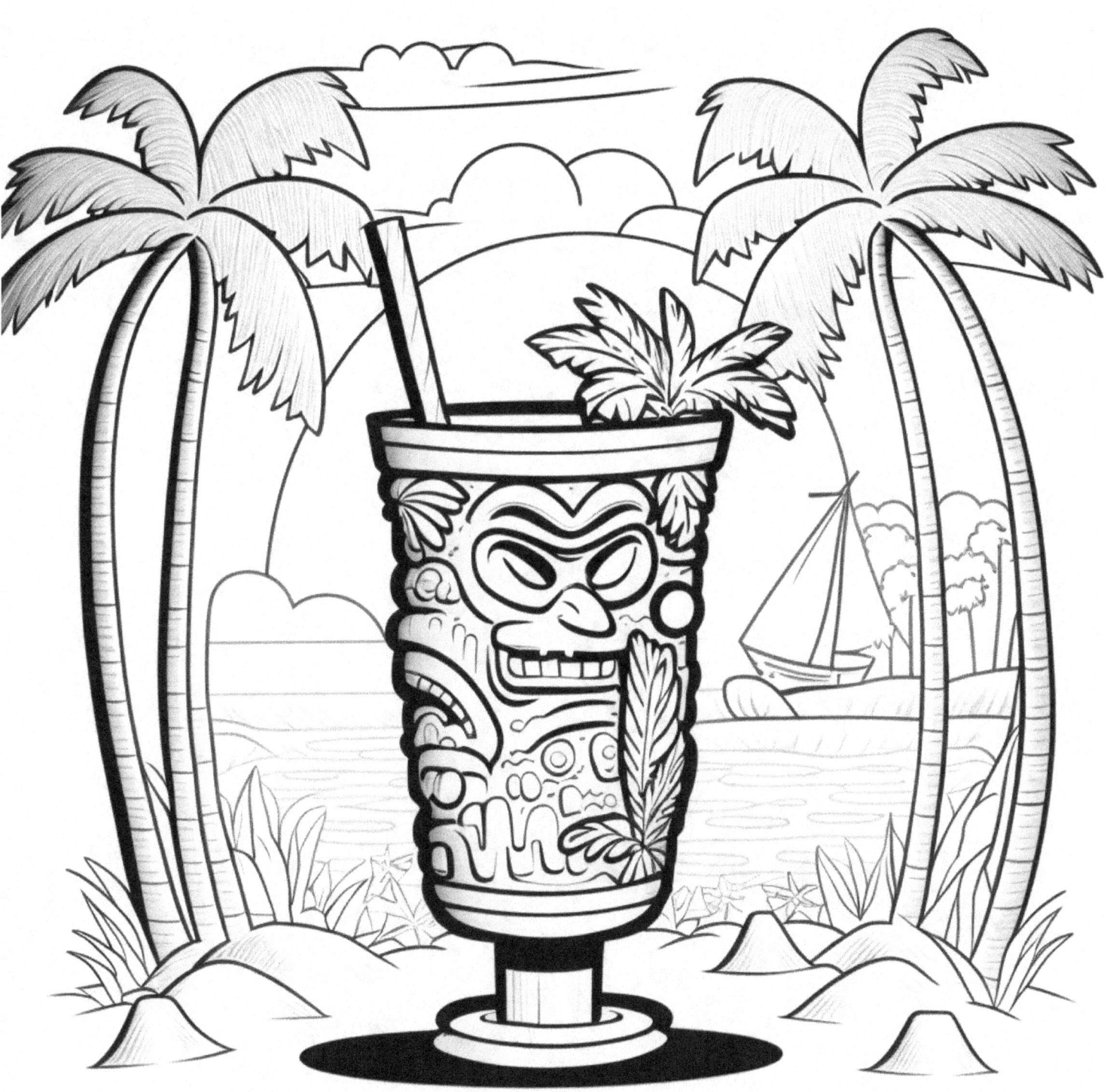

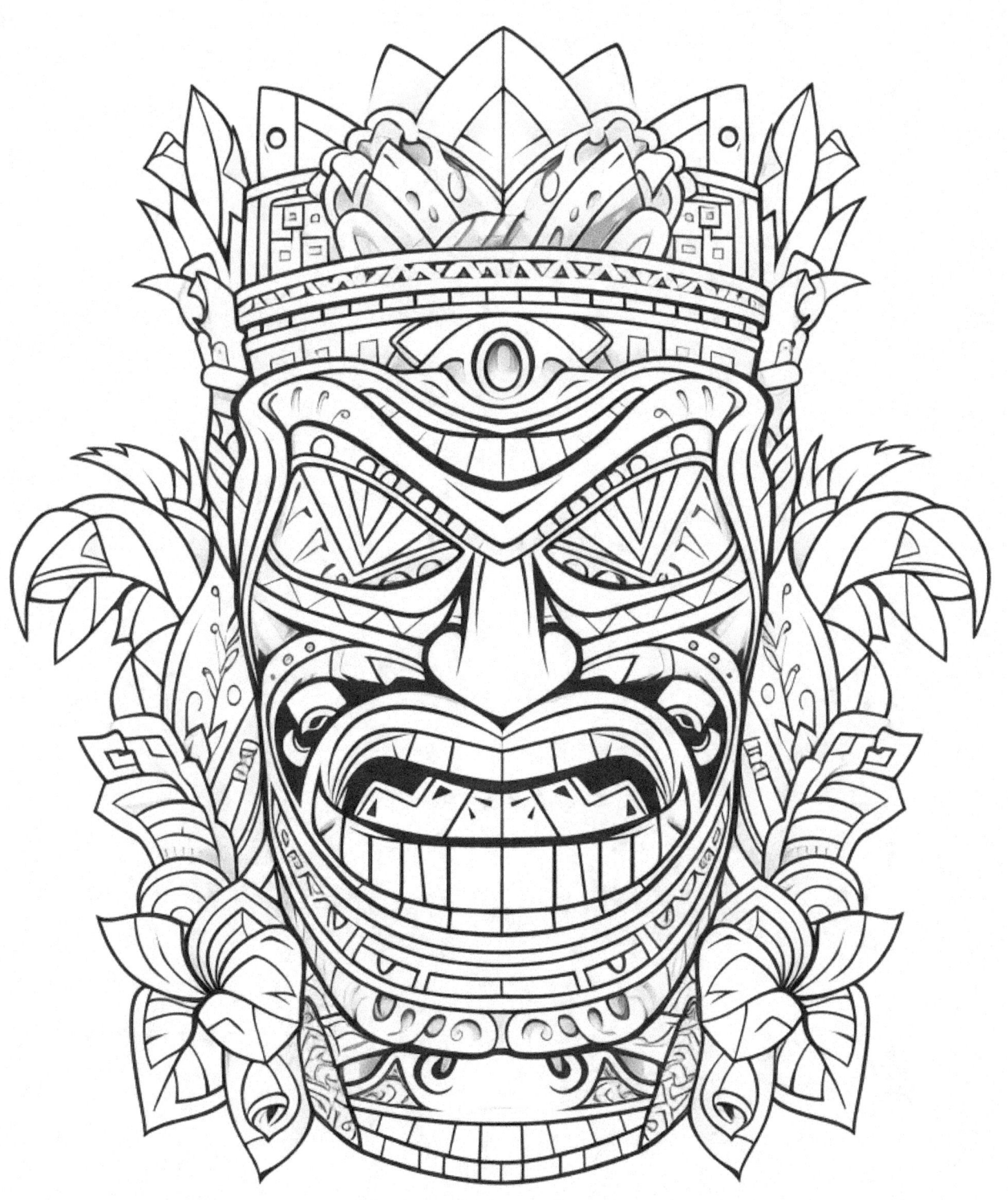

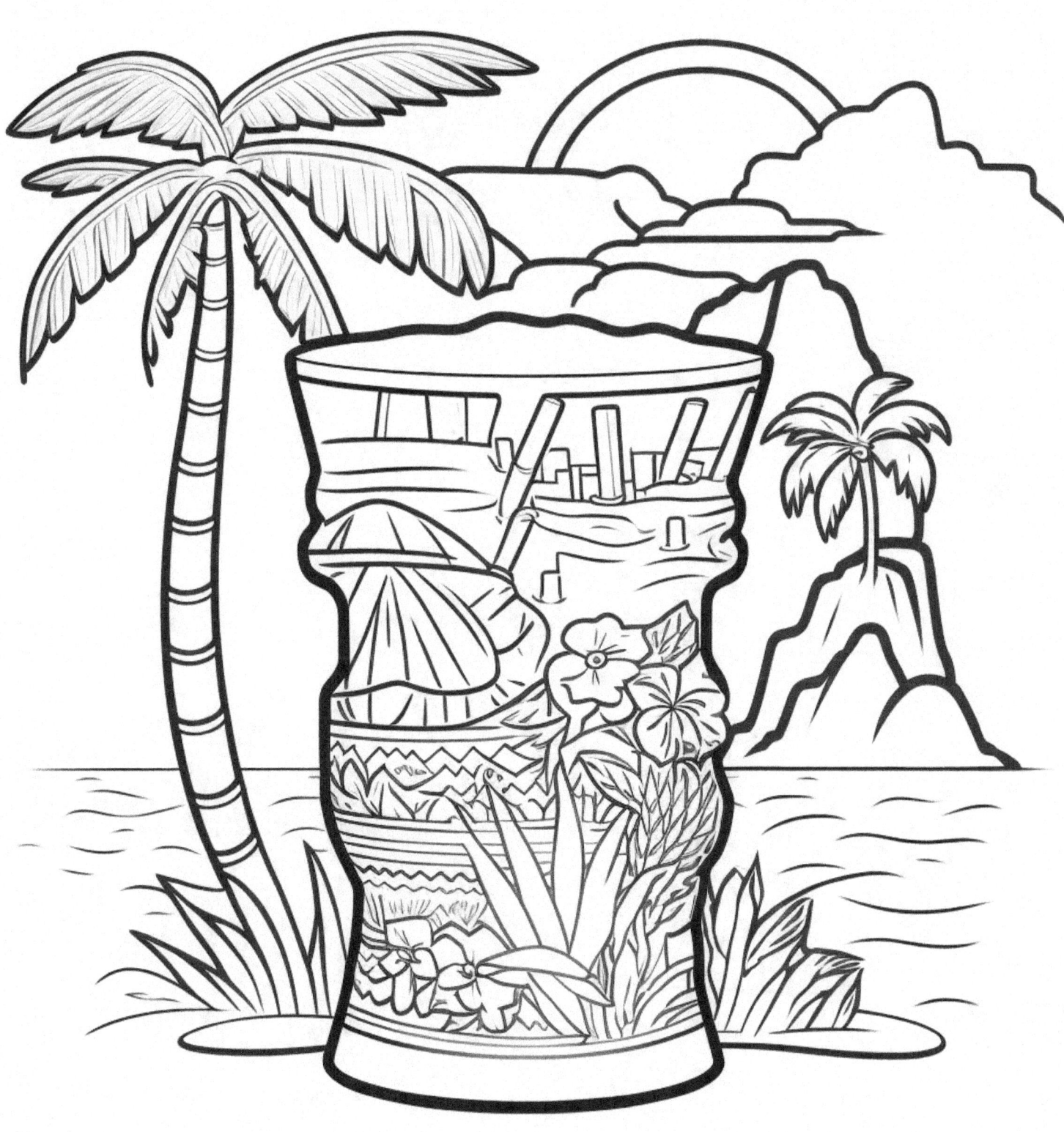

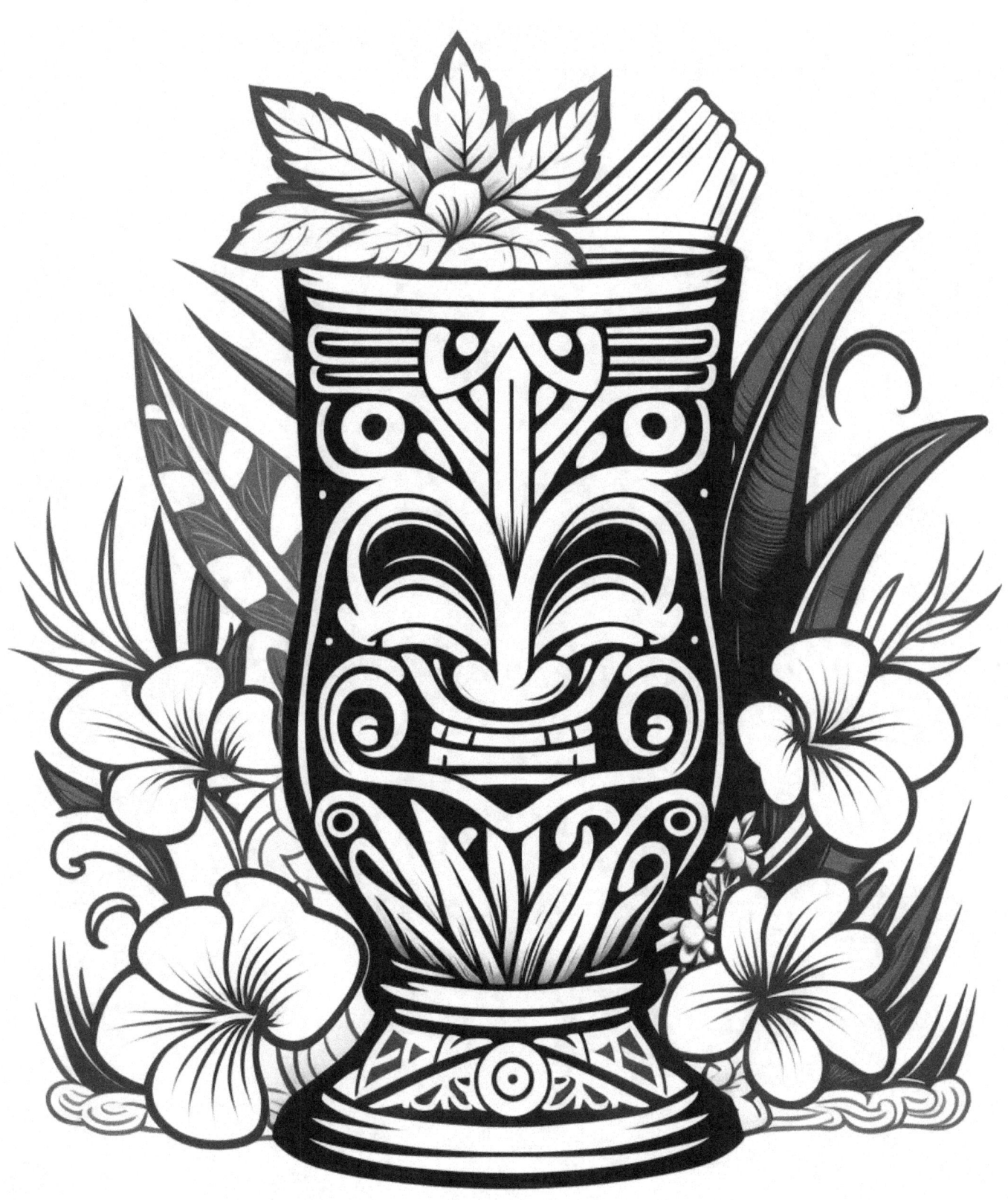

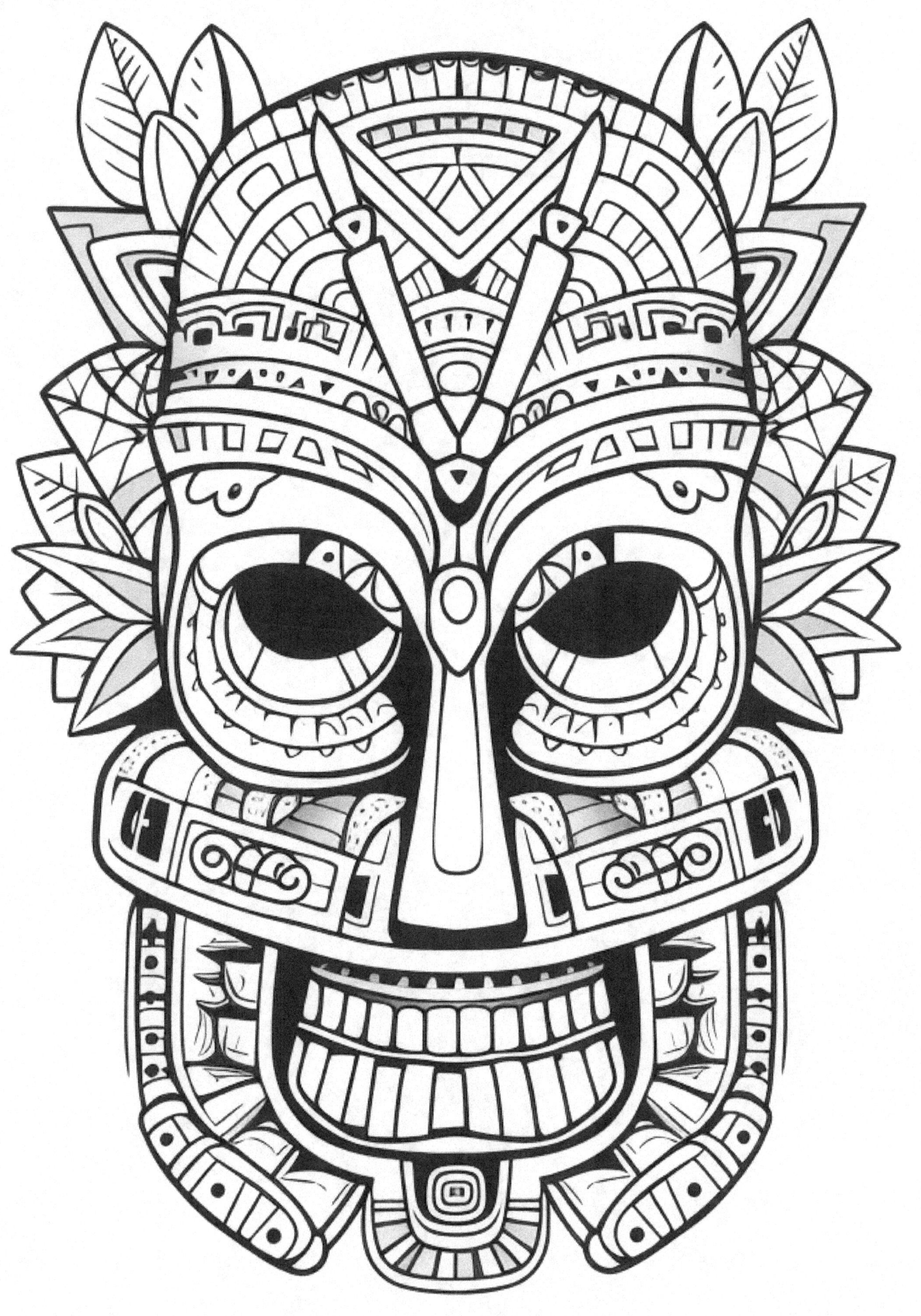

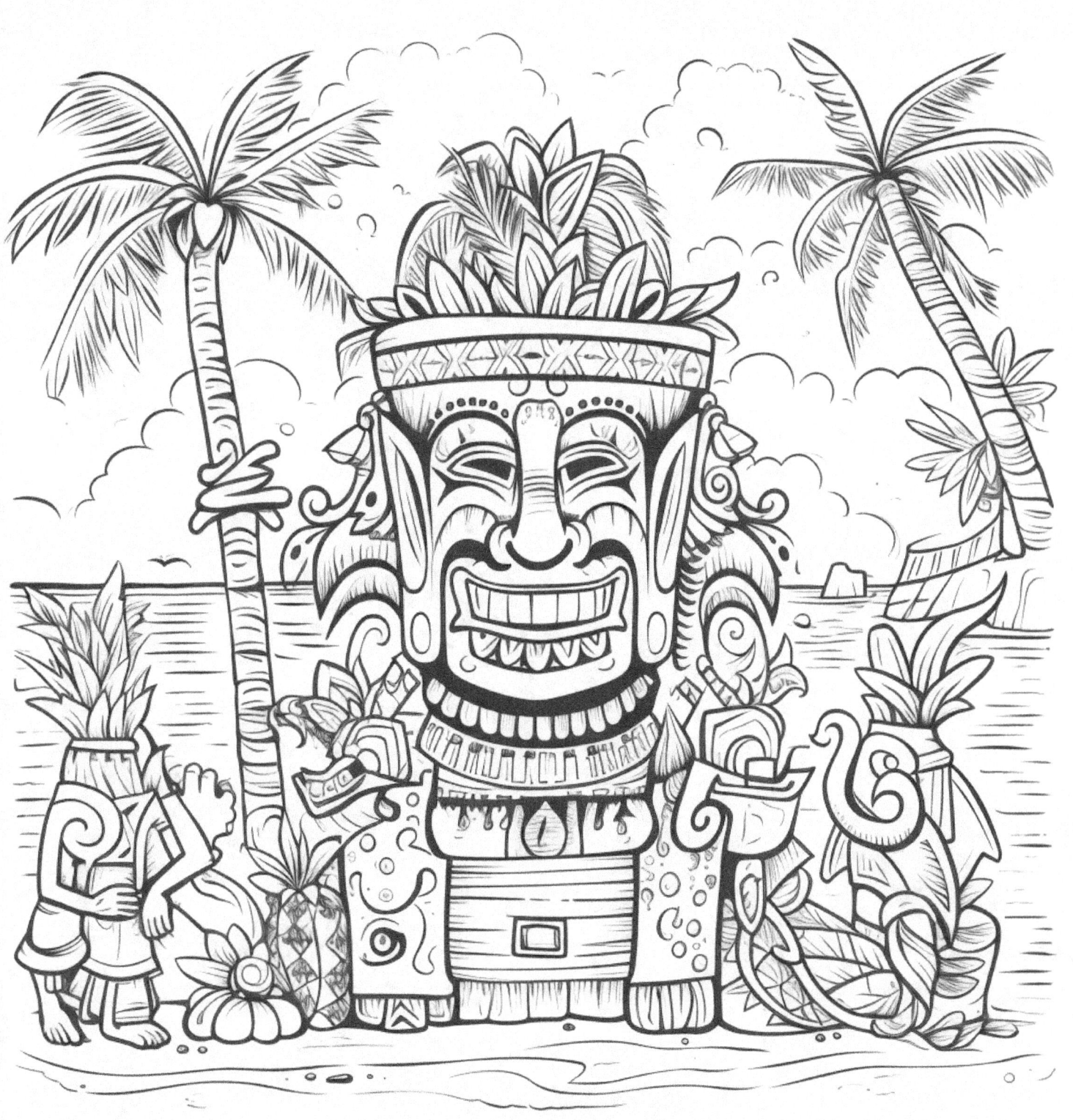

Thank you! Thank you!

Thank you!

Thank you! Thank you!